THE
DARK GODDESS

Dancing with
The Shadow

Marcia Starck
& Gynne Stern

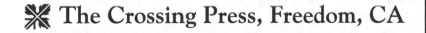 The Crossing Press, Freedom, CA

Acknowledgments

We wish to thank Elaine and John Gill of the Crossing Press for their support and understanding in bringing this book to birth. Thanks also to Claudia L'Amoreaux, our Editor at Crossing Press, Anne Marie Arnold for her design and artwork, and Dena Taylor for her assistance.

For all the women who have sat in circle with the Dark Goddess, we are grateful. To Sedonia Cahill, Jamie Miller, Arisika Razak, and Patricia Waters, who conducted the first Dark Goddess retreat with us at Isis Oasis in 1988, we thank you for helping plant the seed that grew into this book. Appreciation also to the women in Santa Fe who spent time at the Tree House camp the past two summers, becoming intimate with the Dark Mother.

Library of Congress Cataloging-in-Publication Data

Starck, Marcia.
    The dark goddess : dancing with the shadow / Marcia Starck & Gynne Stern.
        p. cm.
    Includes bibliographical references.
    ISBN 0-89594-604-1. -- ISBN 0-89594-603-3 (pbk.)
    1. Shadow (Psychoanalysis) 2. Women -- Psychology.
3. Goddesses.
I. Stern, Gynne. II. Titile.
BF175.5.S55s73 1992

                    155.3'33--dc20 92-40 185
                                  CIP

CONTENTS

To the women in our families—
Margaret Wedge, Margaret Levine,
Helen Cantor, Alice Kassel, and Frances Rosen.

To She who leads us into the cave
of our own darkness and brings us back
into the light of our true being.

3/93

For Judith...
May you continue to
dance with the
Dark Goddess!
Love & Blessings,
Nanna

FOREWORD

The Dark Goddess Dancing with the Shadow is primarily a book about working with the shadow. Although we have used the Jungian concept of the shadow, this book does not represent Jungian thinking nor do we use other Jungian concepts.

Each culture has its "dark" Goddess. The term "dark" does not refer to anything negative but rather implies that which exists before the light; the dark moon phase precedes the new moon. Dark refers to the subconscious as opposed to the conscious, the underworld rather than the world above. Many negative connotations have been associated with the term dark and the color black. Dark has been projected onto people of color; women, especially as regards their sexuality; the occult and healing arts; old age and death itself. Our society has chosen to cover up issues of sexuality, child abuse, incest, rape, and addictions and these are usually referred to as "dark" areas.

The color black is a color of mastery. A black belt is given in the martial arts to those who have achieved a certain level of skill. Likewise, black is used for the final stage of the soul's development in the Sufi tradition. And in the Western world, black is the color of mourning. As a result of the repression of so many of these issues into the unconscious, society has developed a shadow side. Women, in particular, have had to repress much of their intuitive wisdom and sensuality in order to survive. Through using the Dark Goddesses from many cultures, we are uncovering the shadow side of the feminine, and bringing it into the light.

We have selected goddesses from various cultures to work with the different aspects of the feminine shadow on the basis of the relevance of their myths to the parts of the shadow being discussed. Had the purpose and intent of this book been different, we certainly would have included a representative of the African pantheon such as Oya. Oya is involved with the process of death and transmigration of souls after death and a weather goddess related to tornados and winds. We would also have included a Native American Goddess. (Changing Woman symbolizes constant change and transformation, but she is not so much a Dark Goddess as a Nature Goddess.)

There are many other Dark Goddesses whom we would like to acknowledge. Cerridwyn, the Welsh Goddess (her name means cauldron), has been compared with Hecate (there is a song including both of them), and she is certainly important in the Celtic tradition. Hella, the Norse

Goddess who ruled the land of the dead, is related to the German Goddess Holla, Queen of the Witches. (It is interesting that the German world holle is a derivative not only of the word hell, but also holy and heal.) Coatlicue, mother of all Aztec deities, gave both life and death; she is pictured with a necklace or headdress of skulls as is her sister Kali. And no list of Dark Goddesses would be complete without the Irish triple goddess of battle, the Morrigan, or the British Morgan Le Fey, mistress of the mystical island of Avalon.

The Dark Goddess then, is a discussion of the shadow side of the female psyche. To explore the shadow side of the male would require a companion volume utilizing the archetypes of the Dark Gods. However, this is not a book for women only; both sexes need the understanding of the female shadow in order to dance together, just as each of us individually needs to balance our feminine and masculine sides.

It is to this balance, this sacred marriage within ourselves, that we dedicate this book. May we continue to explore the unfolding drama of our shadow. May we continue to integrate the wisdom from our shadow side!

Marcia Starck
Gynne Stern
August, 1992

INTRODUCTION

Light and darkness, the two polarities of the universe, weave in and out of our lives. When the sun appears at dawn we have light; at dusk the sun goes down and the moon appears, casting its reflected light on the earth. As above, so below. As without, so within. Each human personality has its dark (or hidden side) and its light or outward side. The light side, that part that can be seen, is known in psychology as the "conscious" side; the dark or unknown, the "unconscious."

The Shadow

"Who knows what evil lurks in the heart of men? The Shadow knows." Those words at the beginning of each segment of a popular radio program of the 1940s and '50s sent chills down the spines of millions of listeners because they recognized buried within their own hearts the possibility of evil. Everyone has experienced fear of the Shadow, the worry that the dark corner one is afraid to turn might contain a mirror, and that the monster glimpsed in the mirror could be oneself.

Carl Jung used the term "shadow" to represent our hidden side, our darker sister. In Jungian psychology the shadow is always represented by a person of the same sex. It usually refers to a portion of one's being which has been split off remains in the unconscious. The motif of the shadow has been used often in literature—probably the most famous example is in *Dr. Jekyll and Mr Hyde* in which the kindly Dr. Jekyll slowly comes to realize that the murderous Mr. Hyde is none other than himself.

Our shadow can be manifested by someone in the outer world whose qualities seem foreign to us, or by an inner figure, often a character who appears in a dream. An interesting exercise is to examine one's dreams for malign or hostile female figures and then try to understand how the persecuting figure represents oneself and certain inner qualities.

The *personal* shadow contains psychic features of the individual which are unlived or scarcely lived and come from the beginning of life. The *collective* shadow belongs to the collective unconscious and can be personified by a relative or friend, or a literary, historical or mythological figure.

The shadow, usually represented by a negative figure, is a frightening part of ourselves which we do not want to acknowledge often because we were told or trained not to. But the shadow can be positive, particularly when an individual is not living up to her or his potential. In repressed persons, the shadow is often the most alive part of the personality. Only if the shadow is recognized and integrated will a woman or man be able to develop a unified and active sense of self. However, some aspect of the shadow always appears negative—the shadow is too assertive, too independent, too sexual—doesn't act the way a nice girl should. Some of the world's greatest bigots and so-called "do-gooders" are out in the world attacking their own shadow side, often causing much misery in the process.

"Everyone carries a shadow," says Jung, "and the less it is embodied in the individual's conscious, the blacker and denser it is. If the repressed tendencies, the shadow as I call them, were obviously evil, there would be no problem whatever. But the shadow is merely somewhat inferior, primitive, unadapted, and awkward; not wholly bad. It even contains childish or primitive qualities which would in a way vitalize and embellish human existence. Mere suppression of the shadow is as little of a remedy as beheading would be for a headache. If an inferiority is conscious, one always has a chance to correct it. If it is repressed and isolated from consciousness, it never gets corrected."

It is important to note that Jung believed every person had four basic functions: thought/feeling and intuition/sensation. Whichever of these pairs was strongest in the conscious self, then its opposite would lie in the unconscious. The shadow, therefore, is usually connected with one of the inferior functions. For example, Jung considered himself an intuitive thinker; when he had his breakdown he spent three years building a tower on his property in order to heal himself by getting in touch with his shadow side and his inferior sensation function.

The Dark Goddess

Fortunately for women who wish to work with the shadow, most civilizations had one or more goddesses who embodied the darkest areas of the collective psyche. Underneath our veneer of civilization, the same fears and angers beset us that beset our ancient ancestors and can be personified in the deities of many cultures. The dark goddesses functioned as archetypes, taking onto themselves certain traits and thereby cleansing and protecting the populace. An example is the Indian goddess Kali. Kali is portrayed as wearing a necklace of skulls; the skulls do not represent people she has killed but symbolize her role as protector from death. In this aspect, Kali has a cleansing function, helping women to avoid literal death and destruction by enabling them to transform or let go of old patterns of behavior.

In this book we will use the dark goddesses to work with both the personal and the collective unconscious. Often a woman has shoved a certain aspect of her nature into the realm of the unconscious either because she was instructed to do so in her family—"Don't you yell and stamp around like your brothers. You're supposed to be the little mother."—or by society at large which rewards quiet and passive behavior in women.

The problems presented by the shadow in the personal unconscious can only be modified by personal work. Problems of the collective unconscious, however, change somewhat as society itself changes. A girl brought up in the '90s is generally going to feel more comfortable being assertive or sexual than her grandmother brought up in the '40s or '50s because, even if her family tends to be repressive, she will have a certain amount of support from her peers and the mores of society. However, even when the battle seems won on an inner level, the war goes on. Young women constantly complain about "men of the '90s." They talk about men with no commitment, who need women to invite them everywhere, and whose modus operandi is the "disappearing act." In other words, if women insist on being independent or even aggressive, many men retaliate by becoming physically or emotionally unavailable.

Working With the Dark Goddess

One "dark" goddess we will work with in this book is Inanna, who literally isn't dark at all. Inanna is both a human queen and a fertility goddess related to Ishtar, Astarte and Aphrodite. As a human, Inanna makes the heroine's journey into the underworld to visit her sister Ereshkigal, a true dark goddess and queen of the underworld. Ereshkigal is envious of Inanna and puts her to many trials in the underworld, but Inanna, in order to be reborn and reign as queen of Heaven and Earth, must meet these trials successfully. In other words, she must meet her dark sister and undergo spiritual initiation in order to triumph.

Carl Jung speaks of these (underworld) qualities as parts of a Dark Mother archetype. He says that "the place of magic transformation and rebirth, together with the underworld and its inhabitants, are presided over by the mother. On the negative side, the mother archetype may connote anything secret, hidden, dark; the abyss, the world of the dead, anything that devours, seduces, and poisons, that is terrifying and inescapable like fate." [1]

What actually does the Dark Goddess symbolize? The Dark Goddess symbolizes the dark of the Moon, that time before New Moon when there is no light in the night sky. In this darkness our deepest fears become manifest. The dark of the Moon also is the time when many women bleed; thus the Dark Goddess represents Women's menstrual blood. She takes on the aspect of Women's Mysteries that have been feared and misunderstood. She also stands for change and death. The part of our nature that is resistant to change fears the Dark Goddess. Inanna is the spring goddess related to the astrological sign of Taurus. Taurus is the second sign after the spring equinox and occurs between April 20 and May 21. The glyph for Taurus represents the head of a bull; spring represents a time of careless sexuality and fecundity of nature symbolized by the bull. Innana journeys below to meet her sister, Ereshkigal, who represents death and transformation. Ereshkigal can be considered the opposite (or missing shadow) of Innana. In that respect, Ereshkigal is a Scorpionic figure—Scorpio, the eighth sign of the Zodiac, is the opposite sign to Taurus, and represents the erotic power of death. Many dark goddesses, insofar as they represent forbidden sexuality, wildness, transformation and death are related to the sign Scorpio.

There is also a connection between the shadow and the dark of the moon. During the dark phase of the moon, the earth comes between the sun and moon so that the moon's reflected light cannot reach the earth. And the moon, since it doesn't revolve, always has a shadow side that never faces the sun and is never light. So too, do we all have a deeply unconscious side which will never manifest into the light.

Another powerful dark goddess one can use to work with the shadow side is Lilith, the dark side of Eve. Lilith's sexuality was considered dangerous. She was punished by banishment because she was able to say "no" to Adam when he requested she lie beneath him during intercourse, but she was not repentant. Rage is a quality that the Dark Goddess represents. She rages against humanity in her form as Pele, the Hawaiian Goddess, who, when the volcano overflows, destroys all that is in her path. On one level, she is responding to how the earth is being treated and thus cleansing it with the flow of lava. She is also a catalyst for us to give up our attachment to our land and possessions. Sekhmet, the Egyptian Dark Goddess, becomes intoxicated with human blood and rages forth, killing human beings, until a brew of special plants is prepared with alcohol and blood to stop her by deceiving her into thinking the potion she is drinking is human blood. This brew causes Sekhmet to become peaceful and loving, another example of the transformation possible through the Dark Goddess.

For women, using the Dark Goddess in her many forms is an effective tool for working with their shadow side. For men, the Dark Goddess may be used to work with the "anima," the feminine force that resides within each man. (The "anima" and "animus" are terms that were first used by Carl Jung in describing the other half of man or woman. By introducing this concept Jung brought to western psychology the idea inherent in the yin and yang of Eastern philosophy, the polarity within each of us.)

Personal Reflections on Working with
The Dark Goddesses

Marcia:

I first became aware of the Dark Goddess in 1988. She came to me in a dream and told me that it was time for me to work with her. I gathered together a few women with whom I had conducted rituals and suggested doing a Women's retreat focused on the Dark Goddess. We each decided to invoke and work personally with one of the dark mothers.

I chose to work with Pele. I started by invoking her and asking her to speak through me. I found out that some of her rage concerned the taking over of the ancient Hawaiian sacred lands and using them for profit, and not respecting the Kahunas, the ancient Hawaiian priests and holy ones. Pele erupted several times, destroying property, people and all else in her path. I understood Pele, and, in fact, saw that some of my own rage was similar in cause to Pele's. I began to call on her to help me erupt and effectively channel my rage over social injustices. I also began to work personally with Pele to bring out my own shadow side.

To prepare for a second retreat, I invoked Lilith. Lilith's energy seemed familiar to me. I realized that since, astrologically, I had the sign of Scorpio rising at the hour of my birth, I had been engaged with Lilith and sexuality for many years. But I was not aware of her incredible power until the weekend of the retreat itself. Lilith's energy was extremely catalytic for all of us. She brought out some real wildness and deep sensual feelings in the way we danced and expressed ourselves. She also caused a lot of discomfort for some of the participants who were not happy with their own expression of sexuality. Lilith's energy can be very raw and not always pleasant.

Later I began doing one-day workshops with the Dark Goddess in different parts of the country. I was amazed at how many strong issues were catalyzed and how many changes each person went through. (Some of these workshops were also attended by men.) For myself, each time I invoke one of the dark mothers in ritual or in writing, I connect with deeper parts of my own shadow and experience greater wholeness.

Gynne:

I first became interested in working with the Dark Goddesses when I became aware of the power of ritual for bringing to the forefront of consciousness those emotions which are normally repressed or hidden. I have great difficulty expressing anger productively. I grew up with many sexual stereotypes common to those who came of age in the 1950s. Although I rebelled against these sexual taboos, my rebellion only covered up the fact that a great deal of my sexual behavior was a reaction to the Puritanical way in which I was brought up, rather than an expression of my own feelings. In fact, feeling those feelings was very difficult for me, and a lot of my sexuality was play-acting and cerebral rather than life-enhancing. I could see myself as a "love slave," but not as a mature woman who enjoyed her own body.

Although I have had many years of therapy for the above and related problems, I discovered that ritual allowed me the freedom to feel. Assuming the person of the goddess, rather than simply playing a role, did away with personal inhibitions and allowed me the freedom to express openly, both verbally and in action, areas of my life which had been shoved down below conscious awareness. Working with the Dark Goddess in ritual has been a conduit leading to many changes.

ENDNOTES

[1]Jung, C.G. *Four Archetypes*, translated by R.F.C. Hull, from *The Collected Works of C.G. Jung* Vol. 9, part 1, Bollingen Series XX. p.16.

LILITH:

Getting in Touch With
Our Wildness

Invocation to Lilith

I am Lilith.
Not to be controlled.
I live in the wild
with the birds, the beasts,
and the serpents of the desert.
Call on me in lust.

I am Lilith.
Demon, woman,
lover, murderess.
I fly in the dark of night,
steal your children
lie with your men.
Call on me with dread.

I am Lilith.
Irresistible
irredeemable
I have been the consort
of Adam, of Samael, of God.
Call on me for power.

Lilith is the goddess who has never been celebrated as a goddess; the woman who was portrayed as a demon, child destroyer and seductress in Hebrew, Sumerian, Babylonian, Canaanite, Persian, and Arabic mythologies. She is now understood as an archetype embodying the deep sexuality and wildness of woman, symbolizing a central element of the feminine psyche.

Stories and myths about Lilith emphasize her freedom of movement (Marija Gimbutas, author of *The Language of the Goddess*, says that Lilith was descended from the early bird Goddesses). They also emphasize her wildness and oneness with the forces of nature, her independence and refusal to submit to authority, and her deeply sensual and seductive qualities. To understand how we can use Lilith in working with our shadow, we need to examine her stories and myths.

Lilith's Origins

The earliest mention of Lilith is in the Sumerian king list which dates from about 2400 B.C. This list states that the father of the hero Gilgamesh was a Lillu-demon. "The Lillu was one of four demons belonging to the vampire or incubi-succubae class. The other three were Lilitu (Lilith), a she demon; Ardat Lilith, Lilith's handmaiden, who visited men by night and bore them ghostly children; and Irdu Lili, who must have been her male counterpart, visiting women and begetting children by them."[1] Lilith's epithet was "the beautiful maiden" but she was also known as a harlot and a vampire, who, once she chose a lover, would never let him go and refused to give him real satisfaction. She was unable to bear children and had no milk in her breasts.[2] A Babylonian terra-cotta relief shows Lilith as slender and beautiful, with wings and owl feet. On her head she wears a cap embellished by several pairs of horns. In her hands she holds a ring-and-rod combination indicating not a lowly she-demon, but a goddess who tames wild beasts and rules by night.

Other early references to Lilith come from bowls found in Nippur in Babylonia from the 6th century A.D. at the site of a large Jewish colony. These bowls were inscribed and used by the Jews. From a study of the incantation texts on the bowls, Lilith was regarded as the "ghostly paramour of men and constituted a special danger to women during certain times in their sexual life cycle—before defloration and during menstruation," for example. Mothers and newborn babes were especially vulnerable to Lilith and needed protection. A drawing on one of the bowls shows Lilith naked, with long loose hair, pointed breasts, no wings, strongly marked genitals and chained ankles. At night, the female Liliths join men and the male Lilin join women to generate demonic offspring. Once they succeed in attaching themselves to a human, they acquire rights of cohabitation, and must be given a get or letter of divorce, in order to be expelled. [3] Lilith's fame spread from Babylonia to Persia where magic bowls were used to ward off her influence in the same fashion as in Babylonia. Texts on the Persian bowls speak of Lilith in both the singular and plural as female, harmful and dangerous demons associated with male demons and devils. [4]

Lilith in the Old Testament

Lilith, contrary to popular belief, was not mentioned in the Old Testament except once in the book of *Isaiah* relating to the vengeance of Yahweh:

> *The wild shall meet with the jackals*
> *And the satyr shall cry to his fellow,*
> *And Lilith shall repose there*
> *And find her a place of rest.*

Nowhere in the Old Testament is Lilith a part of the Creation Myth or present in the story of Adam and Eve.

The Talmudic Lilith

Lilith is first mentioned in depth in the *Talmud* (the sacred commentaries of Jewish law and scholarship) in the early Middle Ages where we learn more about her life history as it was imagined during this period. Now Lilith appears as Adam's first wife, but they could find no happiness together. Lilith questioned why during intercourse she should lie beneath Adam when, since they were both created from dust she was his equal.

When Adam insisted on the superior position, and Lilith could see he might overpower her, she uttered the name of God and flew away to the Red Sea (considered a place of ill repute populated by demons) where she engaged in "unbridled promiscuity" and bore a brood of more that one hundred demons per day. God sent three angels after her named Senoy, Sansenoy, and Semangelof asking her to return to Adam, but she refused. She did make a bargain with the angels, however, by telling them she was created to weaken babies. With a male baby she would have power over him until the eighth day (the day of his circumcision) and with girls until the twentieth day. However, if she saw the names or images of the angels on an amulet, she would desist from harming the babes and, in addition, kill one hundred of her own children day after day. From that belief came the reason for writing the names of the three angels on amulets and hanging them around the necks of newborn babies.

Lilith in the Later Middle Ages

Later references to Lilith were found in the Kabbalah in the thirteenth century, particularly in the *Zohar* or *Book of Splendor*. (The Kabbalists were the mystics of the Hebrew religion and the *Zohar* is a mystical commentary on the *Old Testament*.) Here Lilith is shown as being created from a husk or shell surrounding the Moon (called a *k'lifah*). According to the *Zohar*, the Sun and Moon were originally equal, but later God caused a separation. "It is fit and proper that the two lights should rule, the greater light by day and the lesser by night. Thus, the dominion of day belongs to the male and the dominion of night to the female. There are two kinds of luminaries. Those which ascend above are called 'luminaries of light' and those which descend below are called 'luminaries of fire.'"[5]

Lilith was created from the lesser light, the Moon. She is reputed to have the body of a beautiful woman from her head to her navel and to be flaming fire from her navel down.[6] Lilith became the consort of Samael, the devil, who inhabited the lower world, while the consort of God was the Shekina (considered to be God's divine feminine presence). As the bride of the Devil, Lilith personifies one aspect of the female shadow. Men experience her as a seductive witch, a strangling mother, and a death-dealing succubus, while women experience her as a dark shadow side of themselves.[7] According to this interpretation, Lilith's refusal to lie underneath Adam was censured because the coupling of Adam and his mate was supposed to represent the sacred marriage of God and his Shekina. In the sacred marriage, woman, as the earth, must lie beneath God or El who represents the heavens, thus conforming to the natural order and recreating the union of El and his beloved Shekina.

Lilith also personifies the natural animal instincts supposed to be found in the feminine. The *Zohar* says that after Adam named all the animals, he had a desire for a mate of his own. Originally Adam was both male and female, but then God put Adam into a deep sleep and severed the female from Adam's side; this female, states the *Zohar,* was the "original Lilith, who was with him and conceived from him."[8]

According to the Old Testament, God created woman from one of Adam's ribs while he slept. Adam called this wife Eve. The Zohar speaks of Lilith as the original female energy that becomes separated from both Adam and Eve. This female energy was prevalent in the goddess cultures and suppressed by the patriarchal writers of the Old Testament. It seems clear that Eve represents the earlier or primary supremacy of the Goddess-based religions before God or El became supreme. The snake is her servant, and she is shown as having wisdom beyond that of the male. (The feminine was originally connected to sexuality, birth and death. With the coming of patriarchal religions these functions were taken over by a male God, and feminine sexuality and magic were disconnected from procreation and motherhood.)

As Hebraic tradition developed, a split developed between Eve, the obedient trusting wife, and Lilith, the instinctual free spirit of woman. However, it is now known that the early Hebrews, at least up until the period of the destruction of the second temple in 70 A.D., worshipped the female goddess, Astoreth or Astarte, because small figurines of that goddess have been found in sites throughout Palestine. Apparently, just as happened later in Christianity, the common people refused to give up their mother goddess and continued to worship her, interrupted only by brief intervals when the Yahwist party in Judaism was successful in temporarily removing her images from the temple. Yahweh means "I am" or "I am being." The Shekina, as God's (or El's) beloved consort had her shrine within the temple or the moving tabernacle. When the second temple was destroyed by the Emperor Titus in the early Christian era, the sacred ark containing the spirit and artifacts of the Shekina was destroyed and scattered throughout the desert, and it was during this period that Lilith returned to become the consort of El, who never ceased mourning his Shekina.

Lilith as Child Killer

In a commentary on the Biblical account of the fall in Genesis, the *Zohar* equates Lilith with the "flame of the flashing sword" that now guards the way to the tree of life. The *Zohar* says, "When she (Lilith) saw the flashing sword revolving, indicating that man had sinned, she fled and wandered about the world and, finding children liable to punishment, she maltreated and killed them." [9]

This quote, plus the story of Lilith's anger at Adam and her subsequent flight to the desert, explains the origin of the belief of Lilith as killer of children in contrast to Eve as mother of children.

In *Symbols of Transformation,* Carl Jung equates Lilith's myth with the myth of Lamia who seduced Zeus. Hera, Zeus' wife, acted out her vengeance by causing Lamina to bring only dead children into the world. Ever since then, Lamia has haunted pregnant women, kidnapped infants, and strangled them.[10] Lilith is the quintessential figure of the "other woman," hated by Hera, upholder of marriage vows. Lilith is desired by men; even if banished from their waking thoughts, she comes to them in their dreams where their desire for her forces them to have intercourse with her and beget her unlawful children. The seductress aspect of Lilith preys on the fears of women regarding the sexual fidelity of their mates. In the imagination of the wife, the other woman is seen as a temptress who often resorts to sexual practices so seductive and exciting that the wife has no chance to rival her. When Lilith refused to lie with Adam because he insisted on the "missionary" position, one implication is that he was unable or unwilling to sexually satisfy women who generally find a lateral or superior position more stimulating. Lilith's flight to the wilderness and her refusal to return to Adam indicate her insistence on sexual satisfaction—a satisfaction formerly thought to be impossible or unnecessary for well brought-up women.

Lilith is associated with the second half of the moon cycle, the waning moon, and with menstruation, which supposedly occurs in the dark of the moon. Eve, on the other hand, is associated with the waxing moon and ovulation. If a woman does not conceive during the first half of the moon, then she bleeds during the second half. Premenstrual wildness and sexuality are associated with Lilith. For some women menstruation is a time of disappointment at not having conceived during the first half of the moon cycle. In this symbolic, but not actual way, Lilith represents the death of the potential child, the unfertilized egg.

Lilith's Freedom and Independence

The story of Lilith's refusal to submit to Adam's will symbolizes woman's desire to be independent from any patriarchal authority. It also symbolizes woman's need to enjoy her own sexuality and pleasure herself during intercourse rather than merely to submit to the will of the man. Passivity during intercourse, or the taking of the inferior position, was seen as a degradation in all Mediterranean societies. In male homosexual intercourse, which was widely accepted in most Mediterranean societies well into the Christian Monastic period, only the passive partner was considered contemptible (unless he was a very young boy). On the other hand, females who assumed the superior position or who wished to please themselves in an active way were often condemned as unnatural, whether they were cohabiting with a man or another female.[11] Females were expected to lie under the man and not control the sexual act. For a man to be manly, whether in intercourse with woman or with someone of his own sex, he had to "stay on top."

Freedom to be oneself and freedom to be equal with men is an important aspect of the Lilith archetype. Barbara Black Koltuv tells us that Lilith represents that quality in woman that refuses to be bound in a relationship. She wants equal freedom to move, change, and be herself. Koltuv equates this with the myth in the *Zohar* where at first the Moon wanted to merge with the Sun, but God sent Her down to follow as a shadow. As a result of this diminishment, the Moon was reborn as Lilith, the fiery free spirit.[12]

Lilith as a Seductress

The *Kabbalah* describes Lilith as a seductress; she is called the Tortuous Serpent because she seduces men to go in tortuous ways. She is also known as the alien woman and impure female. She is said to have left Samael and ascended to Earth where she fornicates with men who sleep alone bringing on spontaneous nocturnal emissions.[13] The *Zohar* states that Lilith returned to Adam who now repudiated her, having vowed to give up all sex for 130 years. Lilith, as usual not taking no for an answer, visited Adam when he slept and mounted him, causing him to have a nocturnal emission. The creatures born from this union were called the "plagues of mankind."[14]

The seductive quality of Lilith was personified by the ancient temple prostitutes who used their sexual powers to bring men into the temples to help them connect with their own anima or female side. In the Sumerian culture, Lilith was known as a handmaiden to Inanna; she gathered men from the streets and brought them into the temple.[15] Oddly enough, during the Hebraic period, most temple prostitutes were men, whose work of servicing barren females was considered holy and necessary to counteract the curse of Lilith. Many Biblical stories of heroines portray Lilith's seductiveness in the wiles of Rachel, Delilah, Esther, Ruth, The Queen of Sheba, Bathsheba, and Lot's daughters. The Queen of Sheba, in particular, is considered a direct incarnation of Lilith.

Lilith Triumphant

Lilith's greatest triumph came with the destruction of the second Jerusalem temple. According to the *Zohar*, the Hebraic godhead was a Tetrad (or four persons in one.) The consonants of Yahweh, YHWH, stand for this tetrad. Y equals the father or wisdom, H equals the mother or understanding, the second W and H stand for two children, one male and one female.[16] Tetrads, although not as common as triads, occur in many religions including Egyptian, Sumerian, early Greek, and Hindu. Jung remarks on the frequency of tetrads in his discussion of the Christian trinity. He felt a fourth needed to be added to the original trio—that fourth being either the Virgin Mary or Satan—either of whom would be the Shadow of the godhead. But it is difficult to attribute a Shadow to the God archetype. So the image of God must be split in twain—a good God in heaven and a bad Satan below.

In addition, God is exclusively masculine according to Christian tradition. If one gives the all-masculine God a dark side containing the opposite of all His positive attributes, you get an identification of the feminine with Satan. God's masculine side is his "ego" or "self" and his feminine side, the Shadow (the devil).

The *Zohar* states that the most terrible outcome of the destruction of the temple and the exile of Israel was that God was forced to accept Lilith as his wife in place of the Shekina. Only the coming of the Messiah can reunite God with his proper bride and bring about the destruction of Lilith. Both Lilith and Samael (the blind angel or blind dragon who is the first angel in heaven and the most Satanic)[17] stand for the feminine side of God. Since God's energy is masculine, feminine energy is considered not only inferior, but potentially evil—an outlook that all Christian and Jewish women learn unconsciously. The doctrines of the Immaculate Conception and the Assumption of the Virgin Mary not only place Mary in heaven, but also remove her typical female attributes—she is the "idea" of the mother, but lacks the body necessary to be one.

Lilith as Wild Woman in Nature

Lilith is always described as a wild woman, living in the desert, close to the birds and beasts. The letters of Lilith's name add up to the word "screech," by Kabbalistic numerology. Wherever the screech owl is mentioned in the Bible, Lilith is implicated. On Yom Kippur, the Day of Atonement, the holiest day in the Hebrew calendar, it is said that Lilith spends the entire day in a screeching battle with Mahalath, a concubine of Samael's. They taunt each other in the desert until their voices rise to heaven, and the earth trembles under their screams.[18] Lilith's screeching may be her attempt to be heard by God or the rage of a woman scorned, or both. It also emphasizes her association with the night, since owls commonly go abroad and screech during the dark hours.

The most familiar representation of Lilith is the one known as Lady of the Beasts. In this representation, a terra cotta relief from Sumer, fashioned around 2,300 B.C., Lilith is pictured with wings, a crown, and the feet of a bird. She stands on a lion's throne in between two lions and holds a staff and a circle, symbols of her dominion over the lions who are associated with the Sun. She is also flanked by two owls, symbols of the Moon and night.

Lilith's wildness and freedom can be experienced by women and men who go out to the wilderness and make animal cries and screams. This allows them to experience not only a primeval part of their own being but also to identify with animals who are free, or sometimes trapped and hunted.

Women in their moon cycle often get in touch with this wildness when they are alone in their moon lodge, free to cry, rage, and give vent to their instinctive side.

Lilith as the Triple Goddess

That Lilith is a descendant of the triple Goddess who existed in Babylonia, Canaan, and Sumeria before the writing of the Old Testament is seen in the story, related earlier, of the three angels, Senoy, Sansenoy, and Semangelof. These three angels possibly represent the three forms of the Goddess —maiden, mother, and crone. The medieval amulets worn as protection against Lilith contain three angels or three birds. Barbara Kultov refs to the three aspects of Lilith in the following way: "Lilith the Younger is Naamah, the maiden and seductress. (According to the *Zohar*, Naamah is another beautiful and seductive demon, although occasionally she appears as a more respectable figure, including as the wife of Noah.) Lilith the Ancient One is child killer, hag and snatcher, while Lilith, herself, is the 'mother of the mixed multitude,' the Goddess of Life and Death, and the flame of the revolving sword."[19]

Lilith, in this context, represents certain qualities of the Great Goddess. She portrays the Lunar consciousness related to the cycles of the moon, death and rebirth; she also portrays the sexual/spiritual connection that was part of Women's Mysteries in the Goddess religions, as well as the instinctual wild side of woman.

Using Lilith to Work with the Shadow

Women use Lilith when their sensuality has been repressed as a result of certain family, religious, and societal pressures, particularly in Western European cultures. Men often use Lilith as an "anima" figure; it is her sensuality and abandon that they cultivate in their own "anima," often dreaming of women who embody these qualities while seeking safer, more motherly qualities in a wife or mate. The "good girl, bad girl" images present in many men's imaginations are individual instances of the split between the Lilith/Eve archetypes.

To connect with their own wildness, men often use the God Dionysus, who symbolizes ecstasy and freedom, in contrast to Apollo's (the Sun God) reason and logic. Dionysus, or Bacchus was the God of wine, and is connected to the Lunar forces rather than Solar ones; in fact, Dionysus had female priests only.[20] If an individual man, or patriarchal society as a whole, buries either one of these images in the unconscious, one or the other will emerge as the shadow, upsetting the social order. Periods of history are often looked at as Apollonian or Dionysian. When one order takes too great a hold over the consciousness of a people, as Apollo did during the 18th century, then we have the sudden eruption of the Dionysian element expressed everywhere from the visionary poetry of Blake, Shelley, and Coleridge to the horrors of the French revolution. The 1960s, too, can be seen as a Dionysian revolt against the Apollonian order and scientific rationality predominant in the 1950s.

Women, by invoking Lilith, often feel strong kundalini energy coursing through their bodies. The kundalini energy, spoken of by the Hindus, is the curled serpent that rests at the seat of the spine in the lowest chakra. When this kundalini is awakened, through various spiritual practices of yoga and breath, it moves up the spinal column. Once one experiences the kundalini energy, it is possible to tap into it and use it. In many cultures in Southeast Asia, this is an energy natural to the female; Hindu art abounds in sculptures and paintings of sensual, voluptuous women. Since this energy has not been acknowledged in the West, it is buried in the collective unconscious and partakes of the Shadow, associated with eroticism, pornography and prostitution.

In, *Pornography and Silence*, Susan Griffin mentions that the sight of a woman's body calls man back to his own animal nature and that this animal nature soon destroys him. As an example, she mentions Eve's temptation of Adam in the Garden.[21] She also gives examples, throughout Western literature, of the male struggle against feminine attempts to weaken men through sex including the stories of Ulysses and the Sirens, Samson and Delilah, and John the Baptist and Salome.[22] For men to gain their life, the woman must die. This has been the role the woman as seductress has played, sapping the life force of the man. The sensual quality of woman has been labeled "dark" and many women out of shame over their "unnatural" or aggressive sexual urges have pushed these desires into their unconscious. One rationalization of why witches were burned during the Inquisition in Europe or later on in Salem, Massachusetts, was that they had the power (gained from intercourse with the Devil) to incite desire and cause impotence in men,[23] connecting these unfortunates to the myths of Lilith we have discussed. The real reasons for witch burning are much more complex, having to do with offering sacrificial victims for various plagues, the desire of men to gain control of women's property, and fear of women's knowledge and healing powers.

Women have gotten in contact with their Lilith nature through various activities. Dance is one important vehicle for women seeking to connect with their sensuality. Several women we know who worked with Lilith started studying Middle Eastern dance, dressing in exotic costumes and moving in sensual ways. They were able to find within themselves a sensuality they had never previously experienced. Others performed African dance and drumming and tapped into a primeval sexual quality. Still others accessed Lilith's sensuality through their voices, chanting from the depths of the solar plexus and hearing their own strong female come through. And some have found Lilith through art and poetry, allowing their unconscious to portray the primeval feminine. Men also can connect with their wildness and sensuality through drumming, song, and ritual. The drumbeat connects them to their instinctual drives and primeval nature. Drumming groups for both men and women have sprung up all over the United States and in parts of Europe.

Women and men who go out in the wilderness backpacking or on a vision quest often manage to tap into their Lilith nature or the Lilith nature in the other. Once this quality has been brought to the surface, it is difficult to lose it again. Women often become freer and more independent after connecting to this aspect of Lilith. Several women have made major changes in their lives after these types of experiences. One left her husband after a marriage of many years because she had forgotten or lost her own identity in the relationship. Her experience in the wilderness brought back her need for independence and freedom. Another woman quit her job as a school counselor and opted for the freedom of running her own counseling practice, living a simpler life style, and spending more time outdoors. A third woman moved to the country with her two children so that they would have a constant connection with nature. Men, too, have experienced change in their lives after working with the Lilith archetype. One man began studying African drumming and consequently experienced much more openness in his sexual expression with his partner. Another left his job as an executive with a large firm, moved to a more rural location, and is involved in leading survival programs for teenagers.

Integrating the Shadow—Eve and Lilith

When women repress their sexuality, cover up their ability to say no, or fear either the wildness within themselves or in others, they have a need to get in touch with Lilith. If the Lilith aspect of a woman remains in the shadow it will usually burst forth in inappropriate ways, sometimes causing damage to herself and others. The movie *Fatal Attraction* portrayed a woman who was so taken over by her sexuality after having a brief fling with a married man that she was unable to let go. When the man rejected her and returned to his wife, she responded in typical Lilith fashion by going after him and his family, including his child, with a large butcher knife. The immense popularity of this movie points to some kind of subliminal recognition on the part of moviegoers of the archetypes embodied.

Women often struggle to integrate their two sides—Lilith and Eve— and both women *and* men often have trouble trying to fulfill both their Dionysian and Apollonian sides. Sometimes women try to integrate these two sides by obtaining their freedom and becoming single mothers. However, children need both male and female energy in their lives, and many single mothers are not able to secure adequate male role models for their children. Although some myths show Lilith as childless and alone, her main representation is as a begetter of multitudes. Nothing in the myth stresses her role as a child rearer, and it doesn't seem particularly useful to invoke Lilith for that purpose as many other goddesses serve as better examples.

One conflict between the Lilith and Eve energies is that between the side of a woman who wants to be a nurturing Eve mother and homemaker and the other side who wants to create or work in the world of ideas and books. Sometimes this conflict is resolved over a period of time. As children grow and mature, the woman becomes freer to enter her deep unconscious and express her creative energies. For the woman playing out her Eve role, Lilith's rage may surface when she herself is tired or sick or her freedom is curtailed in some way by the life she has chosen.

Another way conflict with an unconscious Lilith figures manifests itself is in a woman who is incapable of nurturing her body. Through not being aware of proper nutrition or not being willing to eat well, exercise and use other healthy practices, she may be punishing herself for forbidden, although hidden, physical desires. Abusing the body through drugs and alcohol is one way of allowing oneself to indulge in sexual experiences without having to take full responsibility for one's sexual feelings, allowing the Lilith side to occasionally overpower and destroy the Eve side. Lilith and Eve need to work together so that taking care of the body becomes not a duty but simply another expression of love and sensual pleasure in one's physical being.

There are many ways to integrate Lilith and Eve in the feminine psyche. Perhaps the closest integration historically was in the role of the sacred prostitute. Here was woman using her sensuality in the service of the divine. She expressed her wildness through the ecstasy she experienced in becoming a vehicle for the higher energy of the Goddess, a role to which every woman has a right. Modern woman can express her sexuality in many ways as a vehicle for her spiritual side. Through dance, particularly in certain forms of dance where she becomes the temple dancer, calling the spirit of the Goddess into her body, a woman becomes Lilith and Eve. Through art, music, and poetry women connect with their deeply sensual nature, and at the same time nurture others through their creative spirit. In relationships, both women and men are able to work with their partners so that the sexual aspects of the relationship become a manifestation of the deep bond that exists between two souls. Many study Tantric practices from the Orient in order to become more conscious of sexual practices that serve

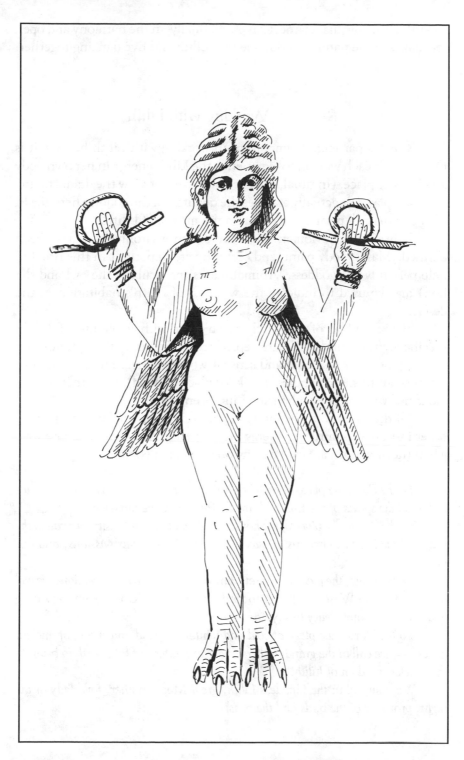

to further the spiritual connection. And, finally, in the harmony and open sensuality of the natural world, one sees Lilith and Eve dancing together.

Ritual for Working with Lilith

Ritual is particularly important in working with Lilith because it is necessary for each woman to experience the Lilith energy in her own body and in a safe place. (In ritual, a participant does not view the drama taking place as a play, but actually assumes the qualities of the goddess herself.) In a Lilith ritual, all participants take on the mantle of Lilith.

To begin, all the women sit in a circle in an environment that has been purified. Masks, body paint, and costumes are important in this ritual to help personify the goddess. Animal masks (particularly the owl and the lion) may be used to indicate the wildness of Lilith's habitation in the desert.

In the middle of the circle is an altar with a picture of Lilith, specifically the Sumerian plate reproduced here, as well as photos and drawings of other beautiful and sensual women. There are owl wings or feathers on the altar, candles (black, or black and red), and other objects identified with night, symbolizing Lilith's energy.

All the women in the circle begin drumming, rattling and playing other instruments until the energy moves in a strong and passionate way. Then the directions are called in by one or more people:

To the East, the place of new beginnings, dawn, and the golden eagle, we call in all the spirits of the East to bring us freedom to be ourselves.

To the South, the place of the hot sun and emotional intensity, we call in the spirits of the South to help us display our sensuousness, our passions, and our wildness.

To the West, the place of sunset, darkness, and deep introspection, we call in the spirits of the West to help us go to the dark caverns and caves of inner knowing and bring forth our ability to say no.

To the North, the place of cold and winter, of wind and snow, of ancient ancestors, we call in the grandmothers and grandfathers of the North to bring us the timeless wisdom of Lilith.

We now call in the Goddess Lilith, great Moon mother, wild lady of the night, protector of the birds and the beasts.

In the first part of the ritual, each person shares the ways in which they would like to be more free, wild, and open with their Lilith energy. In the second part, some women drum while the others move about and dance, expressing their animal and sensual selves in a free way. One person may imitate the owl's sound while others bring forth their own animal allies. Women may dance and move with each other exploring their sensuality together. Nudity, if the weather permits, is a good idea. The taking of psychedelic medicines is discouraged because each woman must first come to her sensuality naturally without artificial aid. All too often women have used drugs and/or alcohol in order to express the sexuality they otherwise would repress. When the dancing and drumming are completed, the participants can share their experience of the parts of them which felt freer and more expressive, or they may wish to silently return to the ordinary world while retaining the freedom they have gained. For women who struggle with sexual or assertive inhibitions, participation in a Lilith ritual would be helpful on a frequent basis.

In the Lilith ritual, women also share the ways they will say "no" to certain elements in their lives. "I will stop catering to my mother's wishes." "I will do what I need to for myself even if my husband (lover) (boss) doesn't agree." "I will stop caretaking my friends." These statements may be written on pieces of paper and thrown into the fire to be burnt as part of the ritual.

Often before closing the ritual, participants stand in a circle, outdoors if possible, where they can see the last sliver of the waning moon. As they do this, they chant and call Lilith into their beings as moon mother.

> *Lilith, Moon mother, great Goddess, be with us.*
> *Lilith, Moon mother, Queen of the beasts, be with us.*
> *Lilith, teach us to be free,*
> *Lilith, teach us to be wild,*
> *Lilith, teach us to be passionate,*
> *Lilith, Lilith, Moon mother, great Goddess.*

Once the circle is closed and the spirits of the directions thanked, dancing and feasting may follow.

Marcia:

My first experience contacting my Lilith nature occurred in my early twenties when I went camping for the first time. Sleeping outdoors, nude under the stars, was a deep way to connect with nature. My body felt free and primeval, like some ancient Goddess, at one with the birds, animals, and insects. I loved washing dishes, using mud to clean them off and rinsing them in the stream. I was brought up to see mud as "dirty," but now I was relating to it as earth and realizing its purity as a cleanser compared with the chemical soaps on the market. Camping and sleeping outdoors gave me my first opening to the freedom and sensuality of my own body.

In my late twenties I worked with a group that utilized Gurdjieff's teachings. We met at a country ranch on week-ends. In the evening, after hard physical work, we would dance outdoors under the open sky. This type of dancing, so free and sensuous and with nature as a backdrop, enabled me to connect deeper with my Lilith side. Prior to this time I had studied ballet, done some ballroom dancing and modern dance, but none of these served to break down my inhibitions and shyness. Later, I studied African and Middle Eastern dance which enabled me to express my sensuality.

As I turned to a study of the Goddess cultures, I found myself deeply attracted to Lilith. It was her qualities of communicating with the birds and animals that I connected with at first, but then as I began to call her in and feel her presence, it was her strong independence and ability to say, "No" that I also found attractive. I realized that I had been doing this in some small way in my own life, but needed to do it more and more out in society with causes that I didn't believe in or support. I also felt a need to make Lilith known and respected, for truly, she has been the only Goddess who has never been given recognition as a Goddess.

Gynne:

Lilith has great emotive power for me mainly because of her insistence in going against what is conventional or expected. Without considering the cost to herself, she defies masculine power whether that of God, Adam, Father or any man. For this defiance, Lilith is willing to pay the price—she is banished to the desert or wilderness; she gives birth to children but is unable to take care of them, she is deprived of the companionship of other women because, since her role is that of the "other woman," most women have been taught to fear and distrust her.

Every woman can use the opportunity to get in touch with the wildness of her own sexuality which is different from that of the sexuality of men. I feel that the Lilith archetype has been created mainly by men and embodies the male dream of the sexual woman, that is, a woman who has as many partners as possible and who seduces men against their will. Now it usually is a male fantasy to have countless sexual partners taken by force (the Don Juan myth) while most women are interested in the quality of the sexual contact, that is multiple orgasms rather than multiple men. Contacting Lilith means to me that women are connecting with their own sexual desires and not with what men want or forbid them to do. Calling on Lilith and using her energy always exacts a price because men have a way of exacting revenge against the woman who is her own authority.

ENDNOTES:

[1]Jacobsen, Thorkild. *The Sumerian King List*. Page 18, n.37, and Page 90, n.31.
[2]Patai, Raphael. *The Hebrew Goddess*. Page 222. Patai cites Eberling and Meissner, *Reallexikon der Assyriologie*, ii,110 as his source.
[3]Ibid. Page 225.
[4]Ibid. Page 228.
[5]From the Zohar I:20 b, as quoted in *The Book of Lilith* by Barbara B. Koltuv. Page 3.
[6]Koltuv, Barbara B. *The Book of Lilith*. Page 4.
[7]Ibid. Page 6.
[8]Zohar i 34 B as quoted in *Koltuv*. Page 8.
[9]Koltuv. Page 2.
[10]Jung, C.G. "*Symbols of Transformation*," *Collected Works*, Vol. V, par.369.
[11]Boswell, John. *Christianity, Social Tolerance & Homosexuality*. Pages 162-3.
[12]Koltuv. Page 22.
[13]Ibid. Page 39.
[14]Ibid, Page 40. *Zohar*, Book I, 55A.
[15]Stone, Merlin. *Ancient Mirrors of Womanhood*. Page 127.
[16]Patai. Page 116.
[17]Scholem, Gershom. *Origins of the Kabbalah*. Page 295.
[18]Ibid. Page 237.
[19]Evans, Arthur. The God of Ecstasy. St. Martins Press, Page 121.
[20]Koltuv. Page 121.
[21]Griffin, Susan. *Pornography and Silence*. Page 31.
[22]Ibid. Page 91.
[23]Ibid. Page 78.

INANNA:

The Heroine's Journey

Invocation to Inanna

Inanna,
Queen of Heaven and Earth,
you travelled underground
expecting to meet
your dark sister,
anticipating
your own death.

Braving dismemberment
Courting extinction
You went in search of knowledge
Into the dark of the earth
Into the depths of the unconscious
reaching for the ever hidden.

Your way to rebirth was through pain.
Your choice was to die in order to live,
to understand all of creation,
to know the dark and the light.
Inanna, Triple Queen
of Heaven and Earth and that Below.

Inanna, Queen of Heaven, and her sister Ereshkigal, Queen of the Underworld, together form a single person, symbolizing the light and the dark, that which is hidden and that which is revealed. Inanna's willingness to descend into the nether realm (ostensibly to attend the burial of her sister's husband Gugalanna) re-enacts the stages of a spiritual pilgrimage, a descent to the dark caverns of the subconscious where the unknown skulks. Inanna's descent is the classic heroine's journey—one that most of us take at some time in our lives. We are *forced* to make this descent when trauma plunges us into depression, when change catalyzes us to make major life decisions, or when physical illness pushes us to look beneath the surface at emotions we have been suppressing. We *choose* this descent when we wish to make contact with the unknown, shadow side of ourselves. When we descend deeply, we transform our conscious self and often radically reorganize our lives. When we choose our own method of descent, we usually have some kind of structure or time frame within which to explore our shadow side and another structure for re-entry into the conscious or upper realm and the integration of the shadow.

Of all the goddesses we will discuss in this book, Inanna, and her darker half Ereshkigal, are the ones who best exemplify the heroine's journey.

Myth of Inanna and Ereshkigal

The story of Inanna begins with a creation myth at a time:

In the first days, in the very first days,
In the first nights, in the very first nights,
In the first years, in the very first years,
In the first days when everything needed was brought into being
In the first days when everything needed was properly nourished

When bread was baked in the shrines of the land,
And bread was tasted in the homes of the land
When heaven had moved away from earth,
and earth had separated from heaven,
and the name of man was fixed;
and the Sky God, An, had carried off the heavens,
And the Air God, Enlil, had carried off the earth,
When the Queen of the Great Below, Ereshkigal, was given
the underworld for her domain.[1]

Notice that mention of Ereshkigal occupies the thirteenth line. In many world mythologies, thirteen is the number of death or, at least, an unlucky or fateful number.[2] In the Tarot, thirteen is the number of the death card. Also notice that Ereshkigal didn't choose the underworld as her realm, but was "given" it.

Inanna, in her youth as spring goddess, rescued the Hullupu tree, which had been uprooted from the banks of the Euphrates during a flood, and took it to Uruk, her city, where she tended and cared for it. From this tree Inanna wished to make herself a shining crown and a beautiful bed.

Nestled in the roots of the tree was a serpent; in its branches sat the Anzu bird; and in the trunk, Lilith lived. Now Inanna wanted to obtain the throne and the bed to consolidate her rule as Queen of Heaven. The snake, the bird, and Lilith symbolize the human qualities of sexuality, greed and lawlessness that Inanna needed to overcome in order to be worthy of her crown and bed. With the help of her brother, Gilgamesh, Inanna rid the tree of its unwanted inhabitants. Inanna's heritage is noble. Her great grandfather, An, the Sky God, had mated with her great grandmother Ki, the Earth Goddess. Ki had a son, Enlil, who raped Ninlil, conceiving Inanna's father, Nanna, the Moon God. An also fathered Enki, the God of Wisdom, who married Ningikuga, the Reed Goddess, and was the father of Ningal, Inanna's mother. Ningal and Nanna mated for love. They had two children, Utu, the sun God and Inanna, Goddess of the Morning and the Evening Star (Venus). Thus, Inanna has one grandmother who was raped and one grandmother and a mother who was loved.[3]

One day Inanna sets out to visit her grandfather Enki, the god of wisdom, who greets her with food and drink. As the two sit about drinking beer together, Enki offers to give Inanna various *me*, or qualities of rulership. He lists eighty *me*, finally ending up with the *me* of making judgments and decisions. Once Inanna receives the *me* of making decisions, she decides to load the *me* onto her boat and take them back to Uruk with her. Although

Enki, when he sobered up from the beer, tried to retrieve the *me* he had given away, Inanna and her female servant, Ninshubur, keep them through a series of clever tricks. Thus, Inanna establishes herself as Queen of Earth as well as of Heaven.

Once Inanna becomes Queen of Earth, she needs a consort. Her family wishes Inanna to marry the shepherd, Dumuzi, but she prefers someone from the grain lineage. Finally she agrees to accept Dumuzi (perhaps indicating a shift from primarily a farming society to a herding one). Inanna falls in love with Dumuzi and the marriage is consummated officially and happily. Their mating is commemorated in a lovely poem[4] reminiscent of the *Song of Solomon*. So happy with Dumuzi is Inanna that she gives him many of the attributes of kingship; however, in male fashion, Dumuzi now wishes to separate himself from Inanna:

> Set me free, my sister, set me free.
> You will be a little daughter to my father.
> Come, my beloved sister, I would go to the palace.
> Set me free.[5]

It is at this point in the saga that Inanna prepares herself for her descent to the underworld on the pretext of attending the funeral of her sister's (Ereshkigal's) husband. The path of descent is traditional, a going into the labyrinth of the earth in order to be reborn on the spiritual plane. Traditional descents usually follow one pattern: 1) separation from home and family, 2) regression to a dark, or pre-natal state, 3) death, dismemberment, suffering, 4) rebirth, 5) sacrifice of another.[6] Without the understanding of the World of the Dead, Inanna's understanding of life is limited.

Inanna prepares herself by gathering together seven of the *me*. These seven *me* are the ordering principles of civilization and are expressed by concrete items of her queenly costume: the "shugurra," the crown which she places on her head; the short lapis beads around her neck; the double stranded beads falling to her breast; the royal robe around her body; the breastplate called "come, man, come" that she wears to protect her chest; the gold ring clasping her wrist; and the lapis measuring rod and line in her hand.[7] Before she sets out, she tells her servant, Ninshubur, that if she does not return from the nether world Ninshubur should beat the drum for her, circle the houses of the Gods, dress like a beggar and pray to Grandfather Enlil. If Enlil doesn't help, then Ninshibur should go to Father Nanna, and if Nanna doesn't help, she is to seek out Grandfather Enki, the God of Wisdom who controls the waters of life.

The underworld is the domain of Inanna's sister, Ereshkigal. Ereshkigal, who was once the grain goddess, formerly ruled in the realm above. Now she has been exiled to the underworld which has become a dreadful place, a land of no return.[8] Ereshkigal doesn't welcome Innana. Instead she is consumed with hate, envy, and jealousy. "In the underworld she [Ereshkigal] has clay and dirty water for her diet. She has no compassion for the relationships of others, husband and wife or parent and child."[9] Since her husband, Gugalanna, the Great Bull of Heaven, is dead, Ereshkigal feels abandoned, unloved, greedy, and full of rage.

When Inanna arrives at the first gate of the underworld, she is asked why she has come. Then Neti, the chief gatekeeper, is instructed by Ereshkigal to open each of the seven gates one by one and strip Inanna of all her finery by removing each of the seven me. First Inanna is deprived of her "shugurra," her crown; at the second gate she loses her small lapis beads; at the third gate, her double strand of beads is removed; next her breastplate is taken away; at the fifth gate, her gold ring is pulled from her wrist; at the sixth gate she loses her lapis measuring rod and line; and finally, her royal robe is stripped from her body. Now Inanna is naked before Ereshkigal. Ereshkigal strikes Inanna and pronounces the death sentence on her, turning Inanna into a corpse, a piece of rotting meat, to be hung from a hook on the wall. Ereshkigal wants Inanna to experience what it is like to be rejected and incapable of movement or relationship.[10] Through this symbolic death, Inanna gains insight into the full cycle of life, pain, and death.

When Inanna doesn't return after three days and nights, Ninshibur contacts Grandfather Enki (after Enlil and Nanna refuse to help her). Enki grieves for Inanna. He fashions a "kurgarra" and a "galatur," two "instinctual, asexual creatures"[11] and tells them to go to Ereshkigal and ask for the corpse that hangs from the hook. One was instructed to sprinkle the food of life on it, and the other, the water of life, so Inanna can be resurrected.

Before Inanna can ascend from the underworld, she must provide someone to take her place. She refuses to give up Ninshubur, her trusted servant, or either of her sons. But when she sees her husband, Dumuzi, dressed in his finery and seated on her throne, she offers him in her place.

Inanna weeps for Dumuzi and mourns his absence. Geshtinanna, Dumuzi's sister, also weeps for him and offers to share his fate. Inanna is able to arrange for Dumuzi to spend half the year in the underworld and Geshtinanna the other half. It is through the love and sacrifice of Geshtinanna that Dumuzi is allowed to return above ground for half the year to fertilize the crops. The Inanna poems all stress the strong love of sister for brother and vice versa. It was Gilgamesh who helped his sister, Inanna, rid the Hullupu tree of the three demons, and it is Geshtinanna who loves Dumuzi sufficiently to sacrifice her own life for him.

Interpretation of the Myth

In order to understand herself, Inanna must go down to the underworld or unconscious realm to meet her darker part, symbolized by Ereshkigal. She must learn that she and Ereshkigal are one being. By attending the funeral of her sister's husband, Gugalanna, she is participating in the funeral of the "great bull" or the masculine primordial energy, the fertilizing power of nature.[12] In Sumer the bull is connected to various local and sky gods.[13] Since Inanna embodies the earth's fertility, the bull symbolizes that energy which complements her. Inanna would prefer to witness someone else's funeral and gain knowledge and power over death by proxy, but in order to enter the realm of Ereshkigal, she must experience death herself.

The relationship between Inanna and Ereshkigal is complex. Ereshkigal lives in the "kur," or the great unknown. Her one great craving is for her own sexual satisfaction. In that way she resembles Lilith who also is compulsive, insatiable sexually, and cannot relate to her offspring. Ereshkigal lives alone, underground, without mother, father, brother, or clothes; her childhood is lost. "She can be considered ... unloving, unloved, abandoned, instinctual, and full of rage, greed and desperate loneliness."[14]

Sylvia Perera interprets Gugalanna as the shadow side of the sky God Enlil. Gugalanna is a rapist and was banished to the underworld for his violence.[15] Another interpretation of Inanna's descent (she is dressed as a bride when she makes her descent in the underworld) is that of a marriage between the new patriarchal consciousness and the older Goddess fertility cults. Elinor Gadon, in *The Once and Future Goddess*, tells us that for the Goddess cultures the underground represented the primal womb, but for the new patriarchal societies, the underworld was a place of horror and dread.[16]

Inanna, when she descends to the underworld, is stripped of all earthly possessions. In a way, she is beginning life anew, starting in the womb, with none of her identities or accomplishments. This reduction of material goods to a bare minimum so that one can connect with her/his true nature is characteristic of many descents. In Native American vision quests, the seeker has a solitary blanket, a pipe and perhaps some water. The blanket is used for warmth at night and as a shield from the sun during the day. The seeker is also confined to a small space, a circle out on the land, far from other humans, where she/he spends three or four days seeking vision.

Another quality of Inanna's descent is sacrifice. Inanna made her journey out of curiosity and a need to merge with her other self, her sister, Ereshkigal. In order to leave the underworld, however, she had to sacrifice someone she loved. In the ancient fertility rites, there was always a human sacrifice to help insure the earth's fertility. Many of the myths follow the pattern of the young God, the Son or Lover, becoming the one sacrificed. This is true of the Egyptian Osiris as well as Adonis (Syria), Attis (Anatolia) and Tammuz (Babylonia). The parallel here is Dumuzi, the shepherd, husband and lover of Inanna, who ends up replacing Inanna in the underworld. In Christianity the same mythic theme occurs through the story of the Virgin Mary and Christ. Christ's sacrifice not only insures the earth's fertility, but signifies redemption of the sins of humanity. Clysta Kinstler, in her novel, *The Moon Under Her Feet,* uses the Inanna descent myth and applies it to the story of Mary Magdalene and Christ. The Magdalene makes a descent into the realm of death, not unlike Inanna, and upon returning, is told that someone else will be sacrificed for her. The sacrifice turns out to be Yeshua, the Christ. This book is an interesting retelling of the Christ story from a feminist perspective that incorporates some of the poetry from the Inanna myths.

Perera sees the Inanna story as an archetypal myth of exchanging energy through sacrifice. The bull of heaven is killed; earth loses its fertilizing principle and is then recompensed through Inanna's death. Inanna provides the food, the fertilizer needed (the rotting meat).[17] Whenever we give up some part of ourselves or take a journey or pilgrimage, we make a sacrifice. We use the forces of nature to reveal to us our dark side— the fears, anxieties—of our own being. Often it is an emotional sacrifice, leaving behind our children and loved ones, to undertake a particular quest or pilgrimage. Always there is an exchange of energy, something we get in return for our sacrifice. Usually this is some kind of spiritual knowledge or wisdom, a deeper integration of our light and dark sides. It is interesting that the Sumerian word for "wisdom" is the same as the word for "ear." Lending an ear means opening oneself up to wisdom.[18]

Inanna and Ereshkigal are two parts of the same being. Ereshkigal has certain qualities that are similar to Lilith's—the powerful sexuality, the deep wounds accumulated from rejection, and relationship to the nighttime aspects of the feminine. When Ereshkigal complains of the anguish of her "outside" and her "inside," the "kurgarra" and "galatur" moan with her, and the pain she feels is assuaged by their concern. She is so touched by their sympathy that she offers gifts. The "kurgarra" and "galatur" ask her to offer that which is hardest for her to give; they ask her to relinquish part of her personal anguish by releasing her nemesis, Inanna. When Ereshkigal agrees, she herself is partially healed.[19]

A better known myth with a similar theme is the Greek myth of Demeter and Persephone. Persephone is taken to the underworld against her will, unlike Inanna who goes of her own accord. Ereshkigal's connection to the Demeter/Persephone myth is complicated. Formerly, Ereshkigal was the grain goddess, as was Demeter. She, herself, rather than her daughter, was forced to inhabit the underworld and, unlike Persephone, was bereft of her husband. Ereshkigal shows all the rage of Demeter in her anger. Probably one reason Inanna ventured below was, as queen, it was her duty to restore the grain each year. Once she made the initial journey, Dumuzi was allowed to take her place.

In Greece, the mysteries of Demeter developed around the cycle of Persephone's abduction and re-birth. These Eleusinian mysteries were related to the seasonal cycle; the Lesser Mysteries taking place in the spring and the Greater Mysteries in the fall.[20] Much of the ritual connected to the Eleusinian mysteries took place at night and was related to the mystery of life and death. Often initiates were kept underground for several days and forced to fast for part of that time.

The Seven Gates of Inanna's Unveiling

Inanna's taking off her clothes and jewelry at each of the seven gates is symbolic of the letting go of old illusions and identities of the self that we depend on. To be naked is symbolic of returning to a state of depersonhood. This is why in prisons and the military, one's clothes and possessions are removed and new ones substituted. Nudity, under ritual circumstances, is the closest physically we can get to our pure being. It represents dropping all masks and personality characteristics.

In the Native American ritual of the sweat lodge (*inipi*), people are also naked (with perhaps a towel for covering). They sit in a dark place, with only the glow of hot rocks and the fire, so that they may connect with their "inside." It is this vulnerability, this nakedness, that enables us to bring up our shadow—the anxieties, fears, and pain which we often hide from ourselves and others. The close environment, the feeling of claustrophobia and even suffocation that can occur, place us at the threshold of the death experience. Will we make it through, will we survive this ordeal? And if we do, how can we be clearer, cleaner, more truthful with ourselves?

The Vision Quest is another experience where we are brought to our nakedness, to the threshold of life and death, in order to see our deep truths rather than hide behind all the games we play out in the world. While vision questing, we wear a thin simple garment with only a blanket to protect us from the elements. Depriving ourselves of food, and, in some cases, water as well, brings us to that same threshold between life and death. And it is at that threshold, that state of consciousness, that our demons are pried loose. The seven garments that Inanna wears, the seven *me*, are worn on her body at the levels of the seven chakras. The giving up of each garment corresponds with opening, or laying bare each chakric center. Starting with her crown, and ending with her robe, Inanna is stripped of all her coverings, and each of her chakras are opened.

The seven gates of the underworld have analogies in other traditions. Erich Neumann describes the seven gates as seven aspects of the feminine.[21] Perera suggests that the seven gates are related to seven planetary positions with which the planet Inanna (Venus) moves into conjunction on her descent and return.[22] While the seven gates may incorporate all these symbolic systems, they are primarily levels of consciousness into which Inanna descends on her pilgrimage into her own unconscious.

The Hero's Journey

Men have no lack of mythical heroes' journeys on which to pattern their actions. They are expected to go forth and slay dragons and win fair maidens, leaving their mother and, eventually, the fair maiden behind while they go on their quests. Gilgamesh, of course, is the great Sumerian hero as well as counterpart and brother to Inanna. However, his story is so long and contains so many adventures, that we'll look instead at the story of Parsifal. Parsifal's story illustrates, as does Inanna's, that the meaning of the journey is to integrate the two sides of the self.

When Parsifal left his mother's home (as all heroes must), he went out into the world, fought and killed the knight who was besieging the castle of a fair lady, and married her. Then, like Dumuzi, he left his bride and went searching for more adventure. He came upon a wasted and terrible land. In the middle of this land was a walled garden with a castle within. Now the lord of this castle was Amfortas, the keeper of the holy grail or chalice which once held Christ's blood. Amfortas had suffered a terrible wound in a battle with another knight—he had been castrated and his wound wouldn't heal. Because of his wound he couldn't take care of the Grail, and the land around him withered and died. The meaning here is that one cannot split off the body from the spirit.

Amfortas could be healed; but only by a person (man) who had no prior knowledge of his wound or even his existence. When Parsifal wandered into the castle he was met joyfully by the attendant knights, and Amfortas was carried in on a litter to meet him. All Parsifal had to do to heal Amfortas was to ask him what ailed him (like Ereshkigal, Amfortas needed to be shown sympathy and concern by having someone inquire sympathetically how he felt), but Parsifal, either because he was a man and hadn't been taught compassion along with jousting, or because he was too shy or too polite, failed to inquire about Amfortas' health and was expelled from the castle.

Parsifal brooded about his failure and sought to re-find the castle for many years, forgetting his wife back home, and wandering the world having many adventures. One condition of finding the castle was none seeking the castle should find it; one condition of healing the wound was that none failing the task should have a second chance.

Parsifal eventually came to a tournament where he fought with a dark knight from Islam. His spear broke against the other knight's helmet, and the Moor, taking compassion on the weaponless Parsifal, refused to fight any longer. The two became friends, and Parsifal became united with his (literally) dark brother or dark self. Suddenly the castle appeared to both knights, they entered, asked the right question, and Amfortas and the surrounding lands were healed. Parsifal became lord guardian of the Grail, and the Moslem married the Grail maiden.

The Parsifal story is particularly interesting because it was written during the Middle Ages when Moors or Moslems were considered infidels and evil. And yet the poem clearly indicates that not only did Parsifal need to meet his own dark side in order to become worthy of the Grail (spirit), but that this dark side could be embodied by a physical person whose color, nationality, and religion were different from that of the Christian Parsifal.

Ritual for Inanna and Ereshkigal

Unless one has had experience in the Native American traditions of the Vision Quest or the Sweat Lodge, the Inanna ritual is an extremely significant ritual for any woman to perform. For women who are timid or who have not been able to assert their authority or independence in the world, the quest part of Inanna's ritual will be the most traumatic and offer the greatest learning experience. For the adventurous woman, meeting with Ereshkigal and being forced to confront the hunger and dissatisfaction in her own nature will prove most beneficial.

Many women can benefit from working with a group that meets twice a month to perform ceremonies at the new and full moon. If one has this supportive atmosphere, the Inanna ritual can be incorporated into one of the meetings, probably during spring (Taurus) or late fall (Scorpio). It would be well to use a location which has access to both outdoors and an indoor room. Or, one can call a special day-long workshop for the specific purpose of experiencing contact with Inanna and Ereshkigal.

Most rituals have a definite pattern which can be observed in various ways. A space is needed for the altar, with the altar cloth placed so that each corner points to one of the four directions, and significant objects can be put on the cloth. The women smudge the area and each other with herbs such as sage, sweet grass or mugwort. Then the four directions are called in with a brief invocation. It is appropriate to pass a "talking stick" or other implement to enable each woman in turn to share her thoughts or feelings with the group. After the sharing, drumming, singing, chanting and/or dancing may contribute to the experience of getting in touch with the goddess(es) invoked. At the close of the ritual, beverages and light snacks are often welcome.

Since the saga of Inanna contains many separate parts helpful to women, we are going to include two separate rituals to invoke her spirit. The first ritual, the descent of Inanna, is a long one and should start in the early evening. All participants sit in a circle and the area is cleansed by smudging. The altar is built in the center with two sections—one for Inanna and one for Ereshkigal. In one section are pictures of Inanna and the other goddesses who are her counterparts: Ishtar, Isis, Venus, Aphrodite, Ashera, Esther. Lapis stones or blue beads may be placed on the altar as well as a crown and gold bracelet. White candles are appropriate on this half of the altar. On the other half of the altar devoted to Ereshkigal are symbols of the darkness and the night— owl's feathers, animal skulls, black candles, bowls of dust, and a glass of muddy water.

The ritual is begun by drumming and rattling to build up the energy. Then the High Priestess or several different people call in the directions:

At the Eastern gate, I call in Inanna, Queen of Heaven and Earth, she who rules over the people of Sumer, and brings enlightenment.

In the South, we call in the love and warmth that the Priestess Inanna had for her consort, Dumuzi, and the love and sacrifice of Dumuzi's sister, Geshtianna.

In the West, we call in Ereshkigal, Queen of the Underworld and the dark places where we must walk carefully and look deeply into our own being.

From the North, we call in the ancient Ancestors who bring us wisdom and guidance for this journey.

When an Inanna ritual has been decided on, it is helpful if all the women participating use the two weeks prior to the ritual to look inward and think about what attributes they value in life and consider what the loss of these attributes would mean. The woman who wishes to become Inanna for the ritual needs to prepare her outfit carefully so that she will have seven objects to discard as she enters into the tunnel to the Underworld.

Once the directions are called in, the drumming and chanting may continue until the presence of the goddess is felt. Then Inanna begins her descent. One by one, the women will remove the seven *me* from her body until, finally, Inanna is left naked in a small room with only a bowl of dirt and a glass of mud. It is here that Inanna will lose her identity as Inanna and encounter her sister, Ereshkigal, her other self. When the Ereshkigal persona takes over, she begins to think about those things in her life that are hardest to give up. As she reaches into herself and discovers those attributes she depends on most heavily—her home, her intelligence, her healing work, her role as a leader or teacher, her family or lover, or whatever she identifies herself with—she will begin to moan. Her "outside," her "inside," her "belly," her "back," and her "liver,"[23] will hurt from loss and deprivation as did Ereshkigal's. This portion of the ritual should take about an hour during which the other women will meet in another space and discuss those attributes they would find the most difficult to give up. Everyone may share imaginatively Inanna's journey.

As Inanna/Ereshkigal's cries become louder and her wailing reaches a crescendo, the women may decide to intervene as messengers from Enki. Their job will be to enter the room and commiserate with Inanna/Ereshkigal and listen to her complaints without censure or judgment. This is not a time for sharing; all attention should be focused on Inanna/Ereshkigal as the women try to hear and absorb her pain. As their listening and empathy become profound, Innana/Ereshkigal will slowly heal and Ereshkigal will agree to allow Inanna to return to the world above ground. Finally the women will ask Inanna to substitute someone to take her place in the Underworld. Inanna's choice must represent someone dear to her whom she loves and would fear losing. This choice is always a serious one and on its sincerity depends much of the success of the descent. When

Inanna has finally chosen, she is led outside, the crown put back on her head, and the women drum, dance, and sing joyfully. Since the descent is a long one, end the ritual festively by serving food and drinks.

Another shorter ritual can be based on Inanna's journey to Father Enki. This ritual is effective for women who have trouble believing they deserve the attributes of power or who feel that they will somehow suffer if they take these attributes away from the powerful men in their lives—their husbands, fathers, lovers, grandfathers, or teachers. For this ritual, the list of attributes or *me* given in the beautiful book, *Inanna, Queen of Heaven and Earth*, by Diane Wolkstein and Samuel Kramer can be read. Each woman chooses those attributes (or thinks up ones of her own) which she feels she lacks or is afraid to assume. In this ritual, after the four directions are called, each woman, one after the other, journeys around the circle and asks for those attributes which she needs. If the women belong to a moon lodge which meets regularly, the group can, at the full moon, discuss their choice of *me* and the successes they have had in using them.

Song to Inanna

I am the daughter of the ancient mother,
I am the child of the mother of the world.
Repeat two lines
Oh Inanna, Oh Inanna, Oh Inanna,
Teaches you who teaches us
To die, be re-born, and rise again,
Die, be re-born, and rise again.
Die, be re-born, and rise again.
I am your daughter, oh ancient mother,
I am your daughter, oh ancient mother,
I am your child, oh mother of the world,
I am your child, oh mother of the world,
Oh Inanna, Oh Inanna, Oh Inanna,
teaches you who teaches us
To die, be re-born, and rise again.
Die, be re-born, and rise again.

(This song was written by Lisa Thiel and is found on the tape, *Prayers for the Planet*, copyright by Lisa Thiel, 1986.)

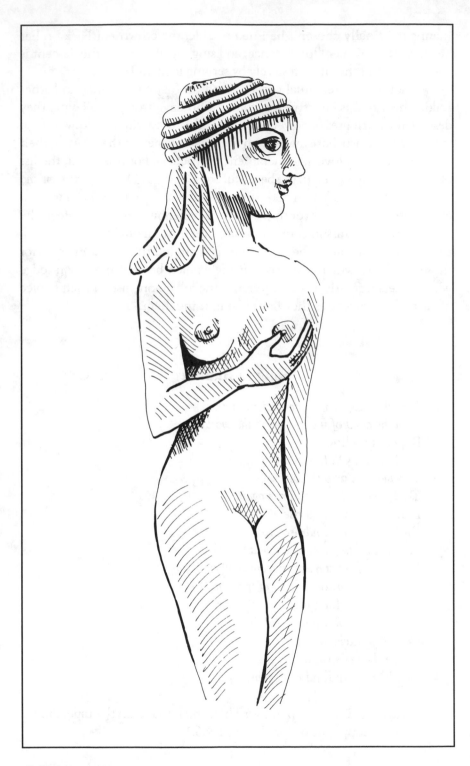

Experiences with Inanna

Marcia:

My own experience with an Inanna ritual started with my first Vision Quest in 1976. It was a rainy September and we were in Bolinas, California, above the ocean. It was extremely windy in addition to the rain. I had purchased a small blue plastic tent at a surplus store just in case of emergency. For the first few hours I spent alone in that tent, my greatest fear was of the elements. I knew I could not stay warm and dry enough if the tent collapsed. I would have to seek someone to help me and interrupt their quest.

After those first hours, I realized that I was, in fact, protected and was there for a greater reason than worrying about the elements. I focused on the parts of my being that I wanted to let go of as well as the parts I truly felt good about. I also went through a series of things that I would want to do if I found out my life were to end shortly. Since I had to stay in my sleeping bag to keep warm, I imagined myself in the womb and being born again. After the Vision Quest, I felt more alive, and had a deeper sense of faith and courage to pursue my path.

In doing the Inanna ritual, I went through the things I have and the attributes I possess and imagined giving up each of them. The first was having a roof over my head and food to eat. I saw myself homeless and with no means of support. That was a very scary one to confront. After dealing with that, I looked at all the wonderful friends and people in my life. What would it be like not to have close friends and people who cared about me? (Since I have lived most of my life alone and not in relationship, the contacts with friends are especially important). I also looked at my roles as a counselor, healer, teacher, astrologer and writer. I imagined giving up each of these, one by one, to see what that would feel like. It was scary to think of me without any of those functions.

At this time in my life as I write this, spring of 1992, I am preparing to move to another state which means leaving behind most of my friends, students, clients, and associates. This move is forcing me to go deeper into the core of my being, as I strip away all those people and places which are familiar to me. Like Inanna, the old clothes and tools will be left behind, but I know there will be other garments waiting when I arrive.

Gynne:

I was born on November thirteen—that is the thirteenth (or unlucky) day of what is known in many European countries as the "black month." Naturally, I feel akin to Ereshkigal; my inner experience has always been that of being thrown into the underworld without the attributes I need to sustain me. The fact that I have lead a very fortunate life and was given by birth and circumstance far more attributes than the average woman can hope for has had no effect on this interior belief. As I worked on this chapter I found myself constantly moaning about my "outside" and my "inside." I also realized that I have avoided experiences of self discovery such as Inanna undertook. I have had a great deal of psychotherapy, but I haven't had the courage to undertake a Vision Quest or even a day at the sweat lodge.

About three years ago, the women in the moon lodge that I belonged to arranged to do a sweat at Kule Loklo, the Mikwok Village near Point Reyes in Northern California. I, of course, decided that I couldn't stand heat, that I didn't want to be crowded indoors with a bunch of women for an entire day, and that the entire experience would be bad for my health. I worried about whether we would be allowed to leave the lodge during the sweat; I hated the idea of being naked or nearly naked with other women who were much younger or in much better physical shape than I was. In other words, I chickened out and didn't attend the sweat. I have always regretted that decision which was the beginning of my leaving the moon group as the women who participated bonded together in a way that I felt left out.

"Feeling left out" is a typical Ereshkigal feeling, and throughout my life I have put myself in the position of feeling that way. It has taken me years to realize that I bring this feeling on myself by choosing not to participate. From the time I was a very small child, I'd say to myself, "They don't want me. I'd better not go. I'll just be in the way. Everyone will be happier if I just don't go." Obviously, I need to work with my Inanna side by taking the attributes I wish for myself and then risk losing them. Working on this chapter has made me decide to risk going on a Vision Quest—something I certainly never planned to do. By calling on Inanna I think I will have the courage to venture into the wilderness on my own for a limited period of time. I can see that without the Inanna/Ereshkigal experience, certain positive changes in my life will be difficult, if not impossible, to make.

ENDNOTES:

[1] Wolkstein, Diane and Samuel Kramer. *Inanna, Queen of Heaven and Earth.* Page 4.
[2] Ibid. Page 139.
[3] Ibid. Page 141.
[4] Ibid. Page 44.
[5] Ibid. Page 48.
[6] Ibid. Page 156. from *Mircea Dismemberment, Myths, Dreams and Mysteries.*
[7] Ibid. Page 56.
[8] Gadon, Elinor W. *The Once and Future Goddess.* Page 130.
[9] Ibid. Page 130, quoting Wolkstein & Kramer, 1983.
[10] Ibid. Page 130.
[11] Wolkstein & Kramer. Page 160.
[12] Perera, Sylvia Brinton. *Descent to the Goddess.* Page 51.
[13] Ibid.
[14] Wolkstein and Kramer. Page 158.
[15] Perera. Page 56.
[16] Gadon. Page 139.
[17] Ibid. Page 55.
[18] Wolkstein and Kramer. Page 156.
[19] Ibid. Page 160.
[20] Harrison, Jane. *Prolegomena to the Study of Greek Religion.* Page 153.
[21] Neumann, Erich. *Great Mother.* Page 160.
[22] Perera. Page 61.
[23] Wolkstein & Kramer. Pages 65-66.

PELE:

Transforming Our Anger

Invocation to Pele

Great Pele,
buried deep
underground.
At the earth's core
your molten anger
bubbles.

Volcano Goddess,
mortals tremble at your wrath.
Incalculable
who can foretell
when your fury
will erupt?

Streams of red black rock
cascading
wind darkly
to the ocean.
Only the sea
cools your rage.

Betrayed
by your sister Hi'iaka,
you showed no mercy
though you carried her
fragile as an egg
under your armpit for safety.

Wrathful Pele,
enlighten us
empower us
by your fiery path.

P ele, the goddess whose spirit dwells within the volcano, Mt. Kilauea on the big island of Hawaii, is fiery, jealous, and vindictive. The hot lava of Mt. Kilauea smolders underneath the earth; earthquakes rock the dark terrain; lava up to 2000 degrees Fahrenheit flows down the mountain's sides, destroying everything in its path. The sound of the molten rock banging against the crater's wall is terrifying. For centuries people have lived on the slopes of this volcano, never knowing when an eruption threatens. Often lives are completely changed and villages wiped out by Mt. Kilauea's action; many who fail to listen to its ominous rumblings choose death rather than leave their familiar homestead.

Anger, the Forbidden Emotion

As natural and inevitable as the instability of the earth's center at the heart of a volcano is the presence of hidden anger in the individual. Some women are able freely to express anger, to "spout off." These women often have a bad reputation and are given unflattering names—"termagant," "harpy," "shrew," "virago," "fishwife"— are only a few of the epithets for angry women throughout the ages. History and literature have many examples of such women—Socrates' wife, Xanthippe, is one such character; Katherine, in Shakespeare's *Taming of the Shrew*, is another. Socrates was pitied or laughed at by contemporaries and historians for having such a terrible wife, while Katherine had to be "tamed" by ill treatment before she became a fit mate for Petrucchio. Although women now are beginning to have powerful positions in the world, the female executive is still expected to be considerate and temperate. If she is harsh or "bossy" she may be derided as pre-menstrual or called a "bitch." In such ways are women taught to keep their anger inside.

Generally, women who express their anger freely and appropriately — that is, directly confront a person or situation—are in the minority. Depression, far more common to women than to men, is often repressed anger. It is "safer" for many women to appear and feel depressed than to be angry. Anger then gets pushed down into the shadow where it erupts or spews forth unexpectedly, similar to the way the volcano blows its top. Unfortunately, hidden anger is a great energy drain, but the chronically tired woman often doesn't know what is wrong with her and blames herself for always feeling tired. Obesity, too, is connected with hidden anger. Fat protects the body from feeling too strongly impinged on from the outside; also, tired women eat for energy. Then as they gain weight, they become angry at themselves for looking fat and unattractive.

Often the issue of anger for women is connected to power. Women, like children, tend to be angriest at physically powerful figures—father or mother, boss, doctor, teacher—and are afraid to express this anger because they are also dependent on that same person for nurturance and love. Children feel that expressing anger towards parents can be dangerous. As babies they learn they can get their wishes for food or comfort satisfied almost instantly by crying for mommy. When they get angry they begin to fear that their angry desire to destroy the parent may also be instantly gratified. Or else that the powerful figure will punish them severely for their angry wishes. Many parents respond to anger in children with anger, just as men often respond to anger in women by physical threats and abuse. The recent movie *Thelma and Louise* showed the various ways in which men will seek and obtain revenge when women step out of line or act on their anger. No wonder women choose depression or illness over anger.

Anger in the Shadow Side of Women

When anger is not expressed, or when the causes for anger persist, anger turns to "rage." Our particular society is full of rage. Women are enraged with men over the way they have been treated throughout history; ethnic minorities feel stored up rage over the way society has abused them (the very term "third world" implies not equal or second class); the poor often rage against those who have material abundance; people who fear sexual activity rail against women's right to choose and the free dissemination of knowledge about contraception; those who worry about the environment and the deteriorating condition of American life rage impotently against the government.

Rage as opposed to anger is never a useful emotion. Many people who feel rage also feel helpless and frustrated. As long as one is enraged, one is either unable to act, or acts destructively. African Americans, for example, who feel enraged against years of mistreatment in this country, are not acting in their best interest when they escape misery and anger through drugs and gang warfare; and whites or blacks who fear the loss of jobs to Asian or Hispanic immigrants lose their own humanity through abusive or "skinhead" behavior. As we write this, the riots in Los Angeles and other cities over the Rodney King decision are taking place. TV commentators wonder why "they are destroying their own neighborhoods." When one feels rage, one destroys what is nearest at hand—an enraged person doesn't stop to think if what she/he is doing is socially or politically useful. Once the initial rage turns to anger, maybe minorities will be able to insist on changing those conditions which caused their rage.

Men and Anger

Anger is not an acceptable emotion for either sex; after all, anger is listed as one of the seven deadly sins. Nonetheless, anger in men seems more permissable than in women. Not only are men allowed and encouraged to engage in institutionalized forms of anger such as war and competitive sports, but their angry outbursts and rages are usually accepted by other men and soothed by women.

In her interesting book on *Women, Sex, and Addiction*, Charlotte Kasl says she spent a lot of time rooting for the Minnesota Twins and observing the behavior of the players. The Twins made a great show of hugging and male bonding, but only when they were winning. When they lost, the players slunk off to the locker room without even looking at each other. Women are used to the job of soothing and consoling. When a woman gets hurt or fails at something, it is natural for other women to comfort rather than ignore her. In this way, women are fortunate. As Kasl says, "For the losing team members to hug and stroke one another would mean admitting to neediness, which is like admitting to dependency on others, and that is something our society discourages in men."[1]

It is important for women to remember that the average man was trained to leave his mother's side early and to fend for himself in the world. Displays of emotion, particularly tears or neediness, are considered unmanly and womanish. A lot of the male shadow has to do with the suppression of traits which are perceived as belonging to women and inappropriate to men. Most men hide their tender feelings in the Shadow. A few years ago, during the early part of the women's movement, when men were encouraged to express their emotions freely, they soon became derided as "wimps."

Cultural indoctrination has made it difficult for women to accept a weeping, hand wringing, ineffectual male.

Anger as Expressed in the Body

Anger in traditional Chinese medicine corresponds to the liver and gall bladder and the element wood. The liver is the largest organ in the body; one of its functions is to detoxify pollutants and other foreign material the body doesn't need. A person with a very toxic liver often turns yellow or bilious (excess bile). Someone whose liver is out of balance appears red and fiery, doesn't handle heat well, and becomes angry quite readily even though that anger often isn't expressed. According to the Chinese, anger is a toxic or excessive emotion resulting from too much fire and needs purifying.

When we invoke Pele in ritual, we are seeking a cathartic experience. Pele is a powerful goddess. Women working in ritual with Pele must expect to encounter disturbing feelings in themselves and in others in the group. For a woman to feel her rage for the first time can be devastating. Most women would rather avoid discovering how angry they are, whom they are angry at, or what they are angry about. Working with Pele in ritual will help us discover and learn to express our anger and rage.

Pele's Origins

Pele originated in Tahiti from a family of seven sons and six daughters born to Haumea and her husband Moemoe. She is described in legends as being very beautiful, with "a back as straight as a cliff and breasts rounded like the Moon."[2] According to some myths, Pele had an urge to travel, so she tucked her little sister, Hi'iaka, who was incubating in the shape of an egg, under her armpit and took a canoe from one of her brothers. Another legend says Pele was expelled by her elder sister, Na-maka-o-kaha'i who was angry because Pele had seduced her husband. Pele traveled with Hi'iaka to various islands including Kauai where she fell in love with the young Kauai chief, Lohiau, whom she determined to take for her husband.[3] Traveling southeast from island to island, she finally came to the Big Island of Hawaii where she was successful in digging deep without striking water, an element not complementary to her fiery nature.[4]

As Pele moved down the island chain through Ni'ihau and Kauai, she dug for her home but she was followed by Na-maka-o-kaha'i, goddess of the sea; wherever Pele excavated a crater, her sister deluged it with water.[5] Since water was believed to be more powerful than fire, her elder sister's pursuit ended in a battle near Maui, and Pele was torn apart. With the death of her mortal body, Pele was elevated to the status of a goddess, as was Hi'iaka. Pele's spirit was freed and took flight to the island of Hawaii where she found a permanent home on Mauna Loa.[6]

Other versions of the Pele myth say that Pele's father was the man eater, Ku-waha-ilo, who dwelt in the heavens. Haumea, her mother, belonged to the Pali (cliff) family. Two daughters were born—Na-maka-o-kaha'i from the breast of Haumea, and Pele from her thighs. Brothers were born from the top of the head of Haumea, her eyes, and mouth, and other children from various other parts. Hi'iaka was born in the shape of an egg and cherished as Pele's favorite.[7]

In another myth Pele sends Hi'iaka to Kauai with her friend Hopoe to bring back her lover, Lohiau. Pele commands them to return in 40 days and not to indulge in any embraces on the way.[8] Many misfortunes befall them, and when they finally reach Kauai, they learn of the death of Lohiau and also of the fact that his body has been stolen and hidden in an inaccessible cave. Hi'iaka scales the cliff and with ten days of incantations, restores his spirit to his body. Their return journey is full of delays, and when the two women reach Pele, she overwhelms them with fire because she is furious at how long they took. When she does this, Hi'iaka, in full view of Pele, lets Lohiau embrace her, although she had fended him off during the entire journey out of loyalty to Pele. Pele calls upon her other sisters to consume Lohiau, but they pity his beauty. She then asks the other gods to help her, but they blow away her flames, and Pele banishes them for disloyalty. Finally Pele herself encircles the lovers with flames; Hi'iaka has a divine body, but Lohiau's body is consumed by fire.[9]

Hi'iaka, Pele's little sister, is the spirit of the dance. Even though Hi'iaka originated in Tahiti, she is considered by Hawaiians to be truly Hawaiian because her egg hatched in Hawaii. Another sister of Pele is Laka, also the patroness of the dance and a goddess of fertility. Laka has a darker side and may appear as Kapo, the goddess of sorcery and dark powers who assumes many shapes at will.

Much of Pele's anger seemed to be called forth by her numerous love affairs. The volcano, Mauna Kea, became extinct because of a furious battle between Pele and Poliahu, goddess of the snow-capped mountain. The battle points out the eternal opposition of fire and ice and suppposedly occurred over Poliahu's success in attracting and seducing handsome young chieftians. Another one of Pele's lovers was Kamapua'a, the hog man demi-

god. Kamapua'a desired Pele who held him off by hurling fire and molten lava at him. Eventually, they became lovers, but were so incompatible that they divided the island of Hawaii between them—Pele taking the drier leeward side where the mountain is streaked with lava flows, and Kamapua'a taking the windward, verdant side. As Pele builds up the island with her lava, Kamapua'a strews the land with his seed, and the rains come to make the island fertile. Many of the small lava formations on the island are said to have been built up by Pele's deluging her unfaithful lovers with lava.

The Meaning of Pele

The myth of Pele and Hi'iaka again brings up the theme of the dark sister and the light sister, different from, but not entirely unlike Inanna and Ereshkigal. Here Pele, the angry jealous, goddess represents the "dark" or shadow. Hi'iaka symbolizes the light through loyalty, compassion, and love. It is Pele who is feared because of her fiery power, and it is Pele who is forced to live underground. When Hi'iaka spends ten days chanting to restore Lohiau's spirit to his body, she is like Geshtinanna, the sister of Dumuzi, who through compassion sacrificed some of her freedom to let Dumuzi live above ground for part of the year.

People in Hawaii sacrifice to Pele so as not to invoke her wrath. It is said that when Pele is angry, she stomps her feet and this starts the eruption of the volcano. In 1880 when Mauna Loa erupted, Princess Ruth Keelikolani chanted the ancient chants and offered gifts to the hot lava streams of Pele. The eruptions stopped the next day.[10] In 1955, when the village of Kapoho was threatened, villagers offered tobacco and food to Pele and the eruptions stopped.[11] Pele has erupted many times since. Visitors to the big island often meet people who have lost homes and businesses to Madam Pele. Living near Pele one must always be ready to sacrifice worldly possessions. This creates a certain kind of psychological state based on constantly being ready to enter the dark cavern of death and destruction.

In 1990 the whole town of Kalapana, which contains an historic painted church, was threatened. The following is from a newspaper article:

"A fiery and terrible end was near yesterday for this community of about 300 people on the lush southeast coast of the Big Island of Hawaii... The wall of molten lava advanced relentlessly, flowing not so much like a river, but inching forward with the power and certainty of a glacier. It was a fearsome sight, one third of a mile wide, as deep as 50 feet at points and leaving, a moving black-orange carpet that snapped giant ironwood trees and utility poles like toothpicks and swallowed roads, homes, cars, anything in its path. By yesterday morning, 123 houses had been burned. It is just a matter of time before Kalapana's last 30 homes, two churches and one store are gone, too, said Harry Kim, the Hawaii County Civil Defense director, who has made a career out of fighting a losing battle against Madame Pele, the Hawaiian fire goddess who rules over volcanoes."[12]

Ritual for Invoking Pele

A cauldron or large pot is placed in the middle of the circle, or the circle is formed around an open fire pit. Wood can be prepared in bundles beforehand to start a ceremonial fire. Remember to have a large pail of water or hose nearby to dampen the fire if it gets out of hand. Since fire and anger are so closely associated, when we call forth our anger it is easy to forget or become confused and let the actual fire rage out of control.

On the altar are pictures of Pele, other fire goddesses, bits of volcanic ash, bright yellow and red stones and crystals, a smudge bowl and a feather fan for smudging.

The ritual is begun by drumming and rattling to build up energy. Then a smudge pot with incense or an abalone shell with cedar or sage is passed around with a feather fan so that participants may smudge each other:

The High Priestess or person officiating calls in the directions:

To the East, we call in the winged ones and the spirits that guard the islands of Hawaii, the sacred land where Pele resides.

To the South, we call in the heat, warmth, passion, and love that emanate from the tropical Pacific islands.

To the West, we call in the deep dark cavern where Pele hides beneath the earth.

To the North, we call in the ancient Kahunas whose spirits guide the energies of Pele's sacred land.

The High Priestess or special fire keeper then lights the ceremonial fire, and each woman twists and stretches to loosen her body, while at the same time moving to mark out her individual space. (For this ritual it is important that each woman define and stay in her own space during the portion of the ritual devoted to movement). All the women then begin to drum, rattle, and make sounds to experience the spirit of Pele. As the intensity increases, the women may jump up and down, dance, throw themselves on the ground, roll around, yell, or scream. (Obviously, this is one ritual where the participants should remember to wear clothing they wouldn't mind dirtying or tearing.) As the women continue to move, they feel the heat of the fire and begin to work up a sweat. Screaming, making loud inarticulate noises, cursing, yelling angry imprecations at someone or something all help to encourage the eruption of anger.

At some point, the High Priestess or leader, through gesture and perhaps music, slowly calms the women and encourages them to rest quietly in their space. Many will continue to groan or talk. The drumming should be stilled. Then the talking stick is passed, and each person speaks of her anger or rage, disclosing at whom her feelings are directed. If a woman has had trouble getting in touch with the spirit of Pele, the group leader can ask her if she wishes to act out her anger through play acting with someone else in the group. Sometimes there is time for only one or two women to work directly on their anger during the sharing part of the ritual. Usually only some women "erupt," and others gain insight by listening to the women inspirited by Pele.

In the last part of the ceremony, the women discuss how they can express anger in their lives, and how they can use this anger for constructive purposes. They can also discuss methods of recognizing when they are angry. Do they get sick? Become passive aggressive and sarcastic? Blow up at times that are inconvenient and hurtful to themselves? Take out their anger on their children or some other non-powerful figure?

After the directions are thanked, the circle is closed, and feasting and dancing may take place with some Hawaiian music in the background. The fire keeper or High Priestess is careful to put out the fire.

Experiences after Working with Pele in Ritual

Marcia:

After working with Pele in ritual I was drawn to the Big Island of Hawaii where I felt Pele's energy in many ways. I was taken on a walk at night on the hot lava and felt her burning up through my feet. I was awed by her vastness and power. Watching the lava flow into the ocean provided me with deep insight into the combination of fire and water, how they can work together and be strong together, resolving the conflict in the myth with Pele and her older sister. (Astrologically I have Mars in the water sign Pisces, representing the oceans, opposite the planet Neptune, the Sea-god. Mars in Pisces is noted for being incapable of showing anger and aggression. Its reputation is that of water washing away the fire; in fact, a big ocean of water. With this configuration in my astrological horoscope, Mars in Pisces opposite Neptune and square my Sun, I have had to work on bringing out aggressive qualities and not holding back my anger. I was extremely timid as a child and young adult.)

I was also taken by a close friend to see Pele's cave, whose location is known only to a few local people. We had to go underground to find it, crawling with flashlights in the coldness of the earth. Upon finding it, I was amazed to see the huge representation of Pele's womb carved in the rock. We sat for a while and meditated near it. One can feel why the native Hawaiians sense Pele to be a mother of this land and worship her as the keeper of it. When one sees her vast opening carved on the rock, one has the sense of an immensely powerful Earth Mother.

A friend of mine felt called by Pele, after working with her in ritual, to go to the Big Island of Hawaii. She had some very strong personal experiences, said she felt more "herself" than she ever felt before. She even buried some of the ashes from her son's cremation near the volcano. (She also has Mars in Pisces and has had to learn to express her anger and dark side.)

About five years ago I portrayed Pele on All Hallows Eve at a weekend ritual devoted to the Dark Goddess. After spending some time at the fire, the group went into a theater to perform individual songs and dances. On my way to the theater, I stopped in my room to get a drum and left some things from the outdoor ritual, including a smudge stick. Later, another woman returning to the dorm discovered the floor of my room was starting to smolder. The smudge stick had burned its way through the bag it was kept in and had already made a small hole in the floor. Also, I had forgotten to put out the fire in the cauldron completely. These two pieces of carelessness, very unlike my usual way of dealing with fire, caused me to think over what had been happening at the workshop. I realized that I was more angry than I thought at my co-leader, a woman I found very controlling. Because we were co-leading this group, I hadn't felt free to explore or express my anger, but kept it bottled inside so that the business of running the workshop could proceed smoothly. Anger is not a wise emotion to neglect when one is invoking the spirit of Pele. Pele forced me to recognize my anger through her own element, fire. Fortunately, someone else, a watery sister, discovered the fire and put it out before it caused serious damage.

Recently, through working with Pele often in ritual, I was able to contact the anger I tend to bury in my shadow side. I had just moved into a new house, and my landlord, another very controlling person, was critical of the way I heated the house. He wanted me to heat my entire house by using a wood burning stove and didn't allow me to use space heaters as a back up. I became very angry with the landlord, and he with me. Through calling on Pele I was able to feel my anger towards this man and express it through chanting and ritual. When the rage towards him subsided, I could then negotiate with him in a rational and calming manner. He agreed to allow me to use the furnace as supplementary heat, and I agreed to learn from him the most efficient way to build and keep the fire in my stove going. What could have been an unfriendly and bitter relationship between two people living side by side, turned out to be a helpful and productive one. Also, I learned that I often respond with rage when I feel controlled by someone else. This knowledge has helped me stand up for what is mine, plus understand and temper my own need to control.

Gynne:

Several years ago I worked in a group counseling situation where we decided to use ritual involving Pele as way of accessing some deep feelings. We did not have a fire available, but we created an altar, called in the directions, and kept the room as warm as possible. We drummed, danced, shouted, and used cloth bats to hit at the floor and furniture. When the time arrived to share experiences, one extremely overweight young woman (Laura) giggled and said she simply was unable to feel any angry feelings. She explained that she never got angry, always got along with everyone, and was considered the jolly person at work who pacified tense situations when they arose. She also talked a bit about her mother (she still lived at home) and how much she liked and got along with her. But, something about her relationship with her mother was bothering her. Our High Priestess gave Laura a pair of cloth bats and asked her to pick out another woman in the group and pretend she was her mother. As Laura's eyes swept the group deciding whom she wanted to play her mother, I remember feeling a start of fear when she looked at me. I was probably the oldest woman in the room, and I suddenly felt physically afraid she might pick me, but she passed me by and chose another woman. As the rest of us drummed, Laura began talking to her mother, laughing and timidly voicing the complaint that her mother always asked her about boy friends and expected to be told about any date or even casual encounter Laura might have with a man. In less than three minutes, Laura was in a rage, shouting and screaming at her "mother" and pummeling her surrogate with the bats. She got so out of control, the rest of the women had to restrain her while the "mother" backed away in horror. Laura, in true Pele fashion, had erupted. Fortunately, she was seeing a therapist and could work on her experience from the ritual through her therapy. That night she stayed at a girl friend's house and shortly after moved away from home. In three years of therapy she had never expressed as much emotion or anger as she did during the Pele ritual.

I, too, tend to keep anger locked deeply in my unconscious. During the ritual I described, I was enough in touch with anger to recognize and fear the rage in Laura when she looked around the room, but not able to feel my own angry emotions. I tend towards passive aggressive behaviors—sarcasm and procrastination are two of my chief ways of expressing anger. When I am out of touch with my feelings, I sabotage myself and others. I attended the Dark Goddess workshop described above by Marcia. I felt unhappy during the Saturday night ritual; in fact, I was the woman who returned to the dorm because I was uncomfortable with the ceremony in the theatre. It is always difficult for me to express myself through drumming, singing and dancing; I have to work at it. That night I resented the work and felt trapped into participating, and generally angry at everyone else enjoying the ritual.

The following day, I got up early, went for a walk, and on the way back stopped in the parking lot to get something out of my car. I then discovered my car key was missing. I looked all over my room, the grass, the dining room—every place I had frequented, but no key. First I managed to completely ruin my car door trying to jimmy the door open through the window; then I spent the remainder of the day sitting by my car waiting for Triple A and a locksmith to arrive. I missed the most meaningful part of the ritual, spent about sixty dollars getting a new key for my car, and had a thoroughly miserable time. Two days later, I received a call from the woman who ran the retreat center saying a maid had found the car key in my bed! This little story perfectly illustrates one kind of problem that can arise when a person refuses to confront the Pele energy when it is invoked. By refusing to take in the spirit of the Goddess and work with it, I set the stage for acting out my anger in a very self destructive and unpleasant fashion.

ENDNOTES:

[1] Kasl, Charlotte Davis. *Women, Sex and Addiction*. Page 229.

[2] Beckwith, Martha. *Hawaiian Mythology*. Page 169.

[3] Ibid.

[4] Ibid. Page 170.

[5] Kane, Herb Kaiwainu. *Pele, Goddess of Hawaii's Volcanoes*. Page 13.

[6] Ibid.

[7] Beckwith. Page 171.

[8] Ibid. Page 173.

[9] Ibid. Pages 173-7.

[10] Stone, Merlin. *Ancient Mirrors of Womanhood*. Page 164.

[11] Ibid.

[12] from the *New York Times*. Robert Reinhold, November 10, 1990.

MEDUSA:

Seeing the Hidden Face
in the Mirror

Invocation to Medusa

Beautiful
beyond desire
Poseidon
bedded you
in his watery nest
beneath the
sea's green waves

Or more intemperate
he laid you down
in Athena's ferny bower
and took your love

You offended
Athena's virgin
grey eyed soul
with your dusky
darkly female presence
so like the sea wrack
so like the sea itself

Now, snakes writhe
about your head
Gold tusks sprout
from your brow
Your mouth is forever
open in outrage
Your scaly body
and repulsive mien
turn all who see
to stone

Women,
look upon
the face of Medusa
She is your sister
She is yourself

Lilith and Inanna both symbolize goddesses who have retained their self determining nature. Inanna was a genuine heroine/goddess. Her myth seems to come from a period when the "mother" goddesses were considered beneficent. Her poems and hymns tell the story of a heroine of divine birth who embarks on a series of adventures during which she outwits her male relatives and her own darker side in order to assume her queenhood. In one of her poems Inanna sings of and rejoices in her "wondrous vulva."[1] Lilith, too, despite a checkered history which lasted from ancient Sumeria through the Hasidic period in the Middle Ages, controlled her own destiny whether as God's consort or as an outlaw in the desert, living with wild animals and giving birth to hundreds of demon children a day.

Medusa has a much more confused story. Norma Goodrich in her book, *Priestesses*, explores all the myths and stories attributed to Medusa, plus, some possible interpretations of other stories which might contain the figure of Medusa hidden within them. According to Goodrich, Medusa was originally a beautiful and powerful African Queen, Mother Goddess, and High Priestess. According to Barbara Walker, Medusa was the serpent goddess of the Libyan Amazons and represented female wisdom. She was the destroyer aspect of the triple goddess which in North Africa was called Ath-enna or Athena.[2] "Her inscription at Sais called her 'mother of all the gods, whom she bore before childbirth existed.' She was past, present and future—all that has been, that is, and that will be."[3] One of her Greek epithets was "metis" or mother. In so far as Athena has been considered to have a mother, her mother's name was Metis (Matris in Latin). The ancient Roman god of religious terror was called Medus.[4]

Considering Medusa's powerful origins, it is interesting that she has ended up primarily known as just another quest on the hero Perseus', journey, very similar to the way dragons were a part of the hero's quest in the Arthurian tales. In fact, Medusa became one part of a dragon or snaky monster, the only human part so that she could be killed, she who was originally terrible because she was a goddess or priestess of death itself. After Perseus managed through trickery to chop off her head, her head retained the power, now used in the service of Perseus, to turn anyone who gazed on it to stone.

The Importance of the Dragon Symbol

Often dragons appear in myths during the change from a Lunar or mother-based religion to a Solar one. King Arthur combined in his ancestry the old religion (son of Uther Pendragon) with Christianity. During his reign, the dragon religion declined, and dragons became perceived as evil, fire breathing monsters to be slain by aspirant knights. The symbol of British Christianity became St. George slaying the dragon.

Again, the German *Nibelungenlied*, particularly as portrayed in Wagner's *Ring* Cycle, tells of the change over from the old Teutonic race of gods to the supremacy of man. Many of the old Teutonic gods have Greek counterparts. The *Ring* begins when Alberich, an evil dwarf, steals the Rhine gold from the Rhine maidens. They curse the gold, saying all who possess it will suffer. Wotan, the king of the gods, is in trouble back home. His wife Frika, angry over his many infidelities (just like Hera with Zeus), has made him build her a splendid new castle, Valhalla. Wotan hired two giants to build the castle and offered them the goddess Freia in payment. Unfortunately, since Freia was the goddess of love (Aphrodite) who tended the apple trees whose fruit kept the gods young, the gods needed her back, and Wotan promised the giants a ring made from the Rhine gold instead. He steals the ring (with the help of Loke, a Hermes-like trickster) and gives it to the giants who, because of the curse, immediately begin to quarrel over who shall possess it. A fight ensues and one brother is killed; the other turns himself into a fiery dragon and retreats deep into the forest to protect his ring.

The German gods, like the Greeks, have an older, female law they must obey. This older, earth goddess has been driven deep beneath the earth, but still is the fate that all, even the gods, must obey. From time to time, this earth mother, Erda, gives Wotan warning, that the possession of the ring will bring destruction to the gods, but he listens too late. Nonetheless, she is the earth mother, or fate, whose laws cannot be breached.

Now Wotan has a favorite daughter, Brynhilde, born to him by Erda, who carries out all his wishes accompanied by her sisters the Valkyries.

Brynhilde is a virgin who belongs only to her father (like Athena) and whose job it is to carry worthy men slain in battle to a special heaven. She disobeys her father in a battle between two mortals, Sigmund and Hunding, helping Sigmund against the express wish of Wotan. For this disobedience Wotan disowns Brynhilde, takes away her immortality, and places her inside a ring of fire guarded by the dragon, to be rescued by a hero brave enough to wrest the ring from the dragon and go through the fire. (Here we have another parallel to Zeus, who disowned Athena when she disobeyed him by favoring the Greeks over the Trojans during the Trojan War). Eventually, Siegfried comes along, kills the dragon, rescues Brynhilde, and they have a brief, ecstatic love affair; but, of course, the curse of the ring continues to work until finally the ring is returned to the Rhine, and then Wotan and all the old gods disappear into Valhalla, never to be heard from again.

We can see how the same themes or archetypes reoccur in different mythologies. The Rhine maidens are another form of the triple goddess; Erda, the earth mother, is the Goddess herself, already in the world of the Solar Teutonic gods, pushed literally underground; Brynhilde is her father's daughter as is Athena—her loyalty is so much to him that she forgets she has a mother; and finally, we have the dragon who plays the role of the fixating parent, guarding the now-mortal Brynhilde from her potential lover, keeping her a virgin and in her daughter state for years.[5]

Medusa bears an interesting relationship to Athena to whom she can be considered the "dark sister" even though we mentioned her before as Athena's possible mother. In Greek mythology, Athena was one of the virgin goddesses; daughter to Zeus alone, she had no mother and sprang full grown and in full armor from Zeus' head. She was Zeus' favorite child. He trusted her to carry his awful aegis (shield), his buckler, and his weapon, the thunderbolt. Athena became one of the principal Greek Solar goddesses. The words used most often to describe her were "grey eyed" or "flashing eyed."[6] Oddly, or perhaps to show her hidden, but still remaining relationship to the Goddess, her bird was the owl. Also, the head on her aegis was that of Medusa.

Medusa represents that shadow side of women thrust upon them by the fears of men. Sigmund Freud, whose work codified and elucidated the fears of men toward their mothers, felt that Medusa's head represented the castrated female genitals. Barbara Walker says one of the meanings of Medusa's hidden, dangerous face was the menstrual taboo—the fear of some primitive men that looking at a menstruating woman can turn man to stone.[7] In one sense, one can view the change from Lunar to Solar religions in Western culture as man's flight from his mother—from the taboos surrounding the sight of menstrual blood, the threat of possible incest, and the omnipresent fear of death or fate.

The fear or dislike men have or have had towards womanly bleeding and female genitalia has been internalized by women into concern about their looks. A recent survey showed that both men and women looked for physical attractiveness as important in finding a sexual or love partner; but only women worried strongly about their own appearance. Men seemed to feel they either fit the criteria of male beauty or that, in their case, beauty didn't matter. Women, typically, worry constantly about their weight, the size of their breasts, fear all signs of aging, and develop illnesses such as anorexia and bulimia which are directly related to dislike of the developing body of the young girl.

Jane Harrison thinks that the story of Athena's birth from Zeus' head was a desperate theological expedient to rid her of her matriarchal origins. Athena is the ancient spokeswoman for father-right. In *The Eumenides*, during the trial of Orestes killing Clytemnestra, his mother, Athena declares:

> This is a ballot for Orestes I shall cast.
> There is no mother anywhere that gave me birth
> and, but for marriage, I am always for the male
> with all my heart, and strongly on my father's side.

Yet on her goatskin tunic or shield, Athena carries the head of Medusa or Metis (ancient goddess of wisdom). In ritual, we hope to reclaim Medusa in order to heal our own separation from our mother.

The Myth of Medusa

Medusa was originally either a priestess or the serpent goddess of ancient Libya—at least there seems to be no doubt she originated in Africa. She was also one of the three Gorgons, children of Phorcys (the old man of the sea) and the Nereid, Ceto. These sisters resided at the western edge of the known world near the Ocean called the Atlantic.[8] In fact the Gorgons were the second set of two trios of female guardian figures relating to the sea. The Graeae personified protection from the white crested waves that dash upon the Mediterranean shore and the Gorgons denote help against the strong billows of the wide open sea at the entrance to the Atlantic.[9]

Originally, the Gorgons had great beauty of face and form and beautiful golden wings.[10] Medusa was the loveliest of the trio. Her black, wavy hair was her chief glory. So exquisite was she that Poseidon, god of the sea, fell in love with her. Perhaps her wavy locks were serpents she entwined in her hair as befitting her stature as high priestess. On her forehead she wore the *uraeus*—Egyptian serpent symbol for Goddess in the form of a rearing cobra, worn on the forehead and representing the third eye.[11] Some thought the lower part of her body was encircled with fishes' scales,[12] although probably the wavy lines on her skirts merely were meant to resemble waves of the sea or the scales of a fish.

At any rate, this lovely maiden, connected with the sea through tradition, hair style and dress, was irresistible to Poseidon. What happened next is slightly muddled, but Athena, Medusa's Solar sister/daughter, plays a major role. Some tales say that Poseidon and Medusa made love in Athena's temple, angering the virgin goddess. Perhaps Athena, despite her vaunted virginity, was jealous of Medusa—this is often the relationship between sisters who have different roles assigned to them by the family. Or perhaps it is the old story of the beauty contest—this time Athena vs. Medusa—that always caused so much grief among the Greeks. Beautiful Medusa was transformed into a creature with protruding tongue, flared nostrils, glaring eyes and curls of venomous serpents. Here we have a perfect example of how the shadow gets constellated and then split off within the personality. Athena didn't like, needed to repress, or was horrified by her feminine side so she turned it into a monster and split herself off from it.

The Gorgons have been described as having the tusks of wild boars for teeth, hands of bronze and golden wings fixed to their shoulders. They were known to turn men to stone just by gazing on them. When Perseus, at the bequest of King Polydectes, set forth to bring back the head of one of the Gorgons, Medusa, as the mortal Gorgon, was the only one whom Perseus could hope to conquer. He had the help of Athena, who naturally wanted to get rid of her shadow side. She gave him a sword and told him to look only at the reflection of Medusa in the polished surface of his shield. He also had the aid of Hermes who led him to the Graeae who were able to tell him where the Gorgons resided. Perseus cut off Medusa's head with one stroke of his blade. From her bleeding neck sprang Pegasus (the winged horse) and Chrysaor (father of a future king of Spain). Perseus put Medusa's head in his wallet (also given to him by Athena) while the other two Gorgons pursued him in vain.[13]

In order to escape from Africa with Medusa's head, Perseus had to kill Atlas. He defeated Atlas only when he showed him Medusa's head, turning

Atlas to stone, and creating the Atlas mountains in the process. As Perseus flew homeward with the head, drops of blood from Medusa's bleeding neck dripped from his wallet onto the earth creating the deadly African snakes.[14] Perseus brought Medusa's Libyan goatskin buckler for Athena to wear as her aegis. In the later trials of Perseus, the head of Medusa turned the sea monster that was threatening Andromeda (another beautiful helpless victim) into stone, and turned Andromeda's former suitors to stone, helping Perseus win Andromeda for his bride.

Medusa, both in her own person and in concord with her two sisters, the other Gorgons, embodied the triple aspect of the Goddess, that of creator, preserver, and destroyer.[15] In her role of preserver, she ruled the mountains and warned sailors away from the fearsome, wild seas of the Atlantic. In a deeper sense, the Gorgons were guardian figures who protected the boundaries of primal ancient mysteries and the threshold of sacred rites. The terrible gaze of the Gorgons which turned men to stone preserved the ancient female rituals.

Transformation and Snake Symbolism

Medusa's transformation from the elegant African priestess with her crown of well behaved snakes (or lovely, wavy hair) to the ugly Gorgon head with hissing snakes personifies the shadow side for many women—the beautiful creative, powerful Goddess versus the ugly death-like face, robbed both of its life force and beauty. Many fear that as they get older, lose positions of authority, are no longer attractive to men, or can no longer bear children, they will become like Medusa. Or many, like Athena, fear their own sexuality, seeing it as a snake-like creature and needing to push it into the shadow.

It is important here to understand the symbol of the snake that Medusa wears on her crown. The snake or serpent has been a symbol of feminine divine wisdom throughout the ages. It also suggests healing power as it is seen in association with Asclepius, the physician, and his daughter, Hygeia, Goddess of health and healing, both pictured with the caduceus or double snakes encircling their staffs. This caduceus symbol is the double helix of the DNA chain, and represents the polarity of the feminine/masculine. Asclepius and Hygeia were associated with the healing centers of ancient Greece where dream incubation was also practiced.

The snake or "serpent power" represents the Kundalini energy in

Hindu religious philosophy. Kundalini is the feminine spiritual principle coiled up as a serpent in the pelvis. She rests at the seat of the spine. Kundalini energy can be awakened and moved up the spine through the seven chakric centers by working with spiritual practices such as yoga and meditation. A Kundalini crisis occurs when the Kundalini awakens too fast and the person doesn't know how to handle the higher energies.

The snake as a transformational symbol is revealed by it shedding its own skin to make way for the new one. Some snakes are venomous and their poison can cause instant death. For these reasons, most people fear snakes. And yet, the antivenin derived from the snake is also an antidote for its poisonous venom.

Death and transformation have always been related as themes throughout literature and mythology. The snake is a symbol of death and also of the transformation that occurs after death or death-like experiences. The Hopi Indians of Arizona do a yearly Snake Dance in which they hold the snakes in their mouths as they dance with them. The idea is that if one can maintain a certain vibration and level of consciousness, the snake will become a friend and not attack. It is as though one uses her/his shamanic powers to tame the snake.

The serpent has always represented the circular (because it bites its own tail), feminine, creative force. Marija Gimbutas, in her encyclopedic book, *The Civilization of the Goddess*, tells us that the snake is the "main image of the vitality and continuity of life, the guarantor of life energy in the home, and the symbol of family and animal life." She mentions folk beliefs in the power of snakes. In Lithuania, on the "Day of Snakes" around the first of February, people prepared various dishes for the snakes and invited them into their homes. If the snakes tasted the food, the year would be prosperous; their choice determined the course of the year. [16]

In Ireland on Brigit's day (February 2), it was believed that the "queen was returning from the Hills"; the queen was a snake goddess.[17] A belief in the magical crown of the snake queen survives in Europe in the folklore. Whoever catches the crown will know the secrets of the world, find enchanted treasures and understand the speech of animals.[18]

Sculptures of the crowned Snake Goddess have been found from Neolithic times starting with the 7th and 6th millennia B.C. in Crete, the Aegean and the Balkans. A net of snakes is sometimes found on her crown.[19] The most widely known sculpture of the Snake Goddess is the one from Crete, the Minoan Snake Goddess from the 16th Century B.C. This Goddess has a crown on her head, her breasts bared, and snakes encircling her waist and arms.

Moses used this magical belief in snakes by creating the serpent, Nehushtan. "And the Lord said unto Moses, make thee a fiery serpent and set it upon a pole; and it shall come to pass that every one that is bitten, when he looketh upon it he shall live. And Moses made a serpent of brass, and put it upon a pole, and it came to pass, that if a serpent had bitten any man, when he beheld the serpent of brass, he lived."[20] The Israelites worshiped this serpent god until the reign of Hezekiah when the new priesthood "cut down the groves and broke in pieces the brazen serpent that Moses had made."[21]

The Christian tradition regarding snakes is quite different. In the Garden of Eden, the eating of the forbidden fruit as recommended by the serpent was seen as evil and a fall from grace; in actuality, it was a fall into consciousness. As we now understand the history at the time the Old Testament was written, the serpent was associated with the ancient Goddess cults where the uraeus-cobra was worn on the foreheads of certain deities (as in the Egyptian pantheon.) The rise of the Yahweh cult brought in a time when priests tried to subjugate or suppress the Goddess and made the serpent a villain.[22] The serpent became known as Lucifer or Satan and a Tempter. Its dark, slimy, underground qualities (alluring and not to be trusted) were equated with the female as symbolized by Eve. Thus did God separate himself his feminine shadow.

The serpent as a representation of evil was also found in ancient Egypt where the god Set was pictured as a serpent. Set dismembered Osiris and fought with Horus and Isis for rulership of the kingdom. Another reference to snakes or serpents was in Central America among the ancient Aztecs and Mayans. The central figure in their mythology was Quetzacoatl, the plumed serpent God.

Two views then emerge of the serpent or snake—first, a symbol of evil and the underground, and later as a holy creature capable of great transformation. The Goddess Medusa encompasses both of these; her beauty and power were seen as ways of luring men; later, her ugliness turned them to stone. Her power also was manifested in her role as a Queen of the Amazons in ancient Libya.[23]

Interpretation of the Medusa Myth

The Medusa myth brings out the conflict between Athena, who, born from the head of Zeus, represented the new Solar gods on Mount Olympus and Medusa, high priestess of a line of Lunar warrior goddesses of Africa.

The Olympian gods sought to rid themselves of the older Lunar goddesses. At the request of Athena, "Perseus overthrew the principal shrine of the old African religion in Libya, and slew the high priestess."[24] When Athena puts her sister Medusa's symbol on her chest, she warns all men that she has no sexuality; that she will not and cannot become sexually involved with men. Unlike Athena, "Medusa's aspects are invariably feminine: children, hair, serpents, fishes, wings, islands, stones, and memorials to the honored dead." When Athena puts Medusa's head on her shield, she attempts to heal the interior split between her masculine and feminine sides.

The myth also suggests territorial rivalry and population expansion. An ancient population expansion in the East caused a war between the Olympian Gods, the Titans and the Gorgons. The myths of Heracles also involve Spain, Morocco and France.[26] Norma Goodrich in her book, *Priestesses*, suggests that Medusa was a warrior queen of the Amazons. She quotes ancient historical sources (Apollonius of Rhodes, Diodorus Siculus) saying that the African Amazons antedated warrior women in both Asia and Greece. "Prominent among the earlier Libyan Amazons was this race called Gorgons against whom Perseus fought. So distinguished for valor were these Amazon priestesses that Zeus was forced to exert himself to defeat them."[27]

Freud, in his 1922 paper entitled "Medusa's Head," offered an interesting interpretation of the themes in the Medusa legend. To Freud, decapitation equals castration. The terror of Medusa is linked to the sight of something so horrible that men will turn to stone. This sight, for Freud, is the female genitals, particularly the mother's, without a penis and surrounded by hair. The snakes, which take the place of Medusa's hair, act as a mitigation of the horror because they replace the penis. In psychoanalytic practice, Freud says it is always assumed that many penises or penis symbols signify (fear of) castration. Also, the sight of Medusa's head turns men to stone—that is, makes them stiff. Again, this stiffening or erection serves to mitigate the horror of castration which is considered a punishment for breaking the incest taboo and desiring the body of the mother. Athena wears the head of Medusa on her breastplate, repelling all sexual desire because she displays the terrifying genitals of the Mother. "Since the Greeks were in the main strongly homosexual, it was inevitable that we should find among them a representation of woman as a being who frightens and repels because she is castrated."[28]

What Freud's speculations mean is women internalize men's horror of female sex organs and displace it to other parts of the body, such as the face, breasts, legs and behind. It partly answers the question as to why women—modern, present-day women—are more concerned about their appearance and have more obsessions and phobias about their bodies than men do. Women, far more than men, find their bodies unacceptable. This feeling has been explained in various ways—for example Naomi Wolf's book, *The Beauty Myth*, talks about the role the media plays in determining what women think they should look like. The discomfort women feel about their bodies is not merely the product of mass media images, but may go deeper into the feeling they have about their own genitalia. Men might worry about the size of their penis, but they didn't seem to be bothered by having masculine genitals.

Medusa is important in her role as the dark sister of Athena. Athena often represents what is noble in woman; the androgynous woman is admired, particularly by feminists. Athena, Hera and Aphrodite were the most powerful of the Greek goddesses. Athens was named after Athena; and its great monument the Parthenon named after her birth. One problem for many feminists is having to juggle relating to men sexually with maintaining identity and power. Too often women feel that in order to appeal to men they must be helpless. Even though Medusa was a powerful priestess, after her head was removed, her only power was passive—the sight of her could turn men to stone.

Ritual For Working With Medusa

The altar is decorated with gold and black candles, snake skins, pictures of Egyptian Goddesses with the uraeus-cobra, pictures of the Minoan snake Goddess and other snake Goddesses, pictures of Medusa, smoky quartz crystals, and black obsidian balls (both symbolizing transformation). Owl feathers (symbolizing Athena) may also be placed on the altar.

Women may wrap colorful African cloths around themselves and wear snake bracelets and any jewelry that has a circular winding effect. Instruments brought to the ritual include rattles that are decorated with snakes and drums.

Two masks should be made before the ritual—one a beautiful Goddess face, and the other an ugly Gorgon—symbolizing Athena and Medusa.

For smudging prior to the beginning of the ritual, copal incense from Mexico may be used.

The High Priestess or four different women call in the directions:

To the East, we call in the dragon spirit who ushers in a new time for re-birth of our feminine spirit,

To the South, we call in the plumed serpent to bring us passion and love.

To the West, we call in the dark black serpent whom we find in the caves.

To the North, we call in the white serpent of wisdom.

And now we invoke Medusa, African Priestess, beautiful Goddess, infuse us with your spirit.

Beginning with the High Priestess or leader, each woman puts on the Gorgon mask and dances out her dark side, the side she fears to look on or to have looked upon; the side she feels is so repulsive that looking on her may turn the onlooker to stone. She then puts on the Athena mask and dances out her creative side.

In the second part of the ritual, all the women dance together without the masks. Then one woman puts on the Gorgon mask and describes her fears of ugliness, loss of power and creativity. If she fears rejection from men because of her aggressive sexual feelings, she can bring this topic up. When she is finished, she hands the mask to another woman who puts it on and describes her feelings. When each has completed this process, one by one, they put on the Athena mask and speak about how they are able to manifest themselves positively in the world and feel their own beauty regardless of their physical appearance and age.

The third part of the ritual is devoted to integrating the Medusa and Athena images. Remember that Medusa (or Metis) means wisdom and is really the mother of Athena. In this part of the ritual we try to integrate our mothers with ourselves—to be our mother's daughter rather than our father's. We call out the name of our mother and try to feel her energy and presence. As each woman, in turn, calls her mother's name, she speaks loudly in her mother's voice, expressing, without censure or praise, her mother's feelings and point of view. As each woman takes her turn, she tries to incorporate her mother into herself; to identify with her mother in a positive way. This part of the ritual ends with all the women drumming and chanting their own names and their mothers' names.

If a live snake is available, it can be very helpful in allowing women to get in touch with the power of their femininity. Each woman who feels comfortable with the snake can hold it and dance with it. At the end, everyone discusses their reactions after feeling or seeing the snake. (If a live snake is used, it is important to understand how to handle a snake. We would suggest that the snake owner be present. Some women may be afraid of snakes. Snakes are delicate creatures not to be carelessly handled, especially by someone who might be afraid.) A toy snake is an acceptable substitute—in ritual hopefully the participants are able to suspend their ordinary belief systems in order to partake in the divine.

Then the women chant together, dance, and celebrate.
Here is a good chant to use:

Snake Woman shedding her skin,
Snake Woman shedding her skin,
Shedding, shedding, shedding her skin
Shedding, shedding, shedding her skin.
Repeat first four lines

Bird Woman taking flight,
Bird Woman taking flight,
Taking, taking, taking flight
Taking, taking, taking flight.
Repeat four lines

Star Woman shining bright,
Star Woman shining bright,
Shining, shining, shining, shining bright
Shining, shining, shining, shining bright.
Repeat four lines

Moon Woman riding the night,
Moon Woman riding the night,
Riding, riding, riding the night
Riding, riding, riding the night.
Repeat four lines

Blossom Woman opening wide,
Blossom Woman opening wide,
Opening, opening, opening wide
Opening, opening, opening wide.
Repeat four lines

Repeat Snake Woman stanza.

(from a tape by Starhawk and the Reclaiming Collective)

Personal Experiences With Medusa

Marcia:

In my early twenties I was in therapy with a man who owned a snake. I saw the snake and saw how gently my therapist held it. Later he asked my ex-husband, who was a carpenter, to build a cage for the snake. My ex-husband learned a lot about handling snakes when he built this cage. At the time, I was too afraid to hold the snake. I was nervous and not very centered. But I felt the power of the snake and desired the quality which would enable me to hold it and learn from it.

Many years later I went with a friend to visit an older spiritual man in New Mexico. We had decided to arrive at 11 A.M. on a Tuesday morning. After we arrived, he asked if we would like to go out to the kiva to see it and do a ritual. We were both excited to do this. Then he told us that just that morning, a few hours before we arrived, an old friend of his had appeared whom he hadn't seen in a year; the friend was a snake!

He asked if we would mind if this friend joined us in the ritual. We both agreed that this would be fine, each of us feeling that we might get to hold the snake. I felt ready for this if it was to happen. However, the man we were visiting carried the snake to the kiva and put the snake in a cage there. So we never did get to hold him. I think I felt somewhat disappointed and yet at the same time interested in the snake and why he would show up at the same time we did. This had been our host's feeling as well.

I realized what an important symbol the snake was for me, personally, having the sign Scorpio rising in my horoscope. Scorpio suggests death and regeneration, constant transformations. Then at the first Dark Goddess retreat I sponsored, one of my friends worked with Medusa and brought her spirit through. She became enraged at "that wimp Perseus" and for the first time, I understood the true meaning of the Medusa myth. Medusa became for me a symbol of one whose power, authority, creativity and beauty are taken away.

As I began to work with Medusa in ritual, I saw how many women identified with her in some way. For me, using both the masks brought on issues related to my hair which has always been very thick and somewhat unmanageable. When I was very young I had long braids; then my mother cut these off and I was quite upset. Later, as I grew into my own power, I let my hair grow long again, which I liked, though it was a challenge to keep it looking nice. My family, however, always criticized me when my hair was not short. So my hair became my main issue for asserting my own power and also determined how I felt about the way I looked. I went through stages of cutting it shorter to experiment and to become unattached to its length, but, ultimately, I have always let it grow back. Understanding Medusa's crown with the net of snakes provided me with some real insights on my issue with my hair.

Gynne:

Although I have never worked with Medusa in ritual, I realized when writing this chapter that I was strongly moved by the Medusa myth without personally being able to identify with either Athena or Medusa. Then I remembered that the Medusa myth, like those of Inanna and Pele, has a third feminine force present—that of Andromeda. Andromeda was a hapless princess chained to a rock somewhere in the Mediterranean. Heavy waves crashed against the rock and threatened to engulf her. At her feet a sea monster thrashed and snapped, expecting to devour her. Andromeda could only cling to her rock, shrinking back from the sea and its monster, waiting for the hero to rescue her. And the hero, Perseus, did come. But he was not interested in Andromeda. His interests were in his own prowess and cunning, and in pleasing the king (Andromeda's father) who had set him this task.

I think this story of the helpless woman waiting for the man to rescue her expresses the plight of many females, including, somewhat unconsciously, my own. Unable to identify with the self-sufficient androgyny of Athena and unwilling to align herself with the threatening feminine, but frozen, sexuality of Medusa, she has no choice except to remain the maiden waiting for rescue, fearful of being drowned (return to the mother) or eaten by the sea monster (rape by the male). The Medusa story contains the triple aspect of the goddess, here divided not by age, but by function. Athena represents the creative, active principle associated with the father; Medusa the repressed and denied wisdom of the mother (Metis); and Andromeda the helplessness of the maiden waiting to be reclaimed by the mother or stolen by the underworld (see also the story of Persephone).

Christine Downing in Goddess says, "The power that fathers have for their daughters lies at the very heart of patriarchal culture. Indeed, we might say that the patriarch appears when the daughter is felt to belong and feels herself to belong to the father, for the son's identification with the father does not imply the *same radical devaluation of mother-right*. To understand ourselves as women in a patriarchally-ordered world... means trying to comprehend as fully as we can how our creativity is released, distorted, and inhibited by the power of the father—not primarily his outward power, but his power in our own imagination.(emphasis mine)"[29] I feel it is very important for women to recognize how they contribute to the patriarchy, because until they do, the patriarchy will continue in its present form. Ritually reuniting Medusa with Metis (who is really Athena), that is, reuniting Medusa with herself, points the way for women to act in a powerful way.

I like very much the poem by May Sarton, quoted by Downing in her book. The feelings expressed are those we hope to contact in the ritual.

> *I saw you once, Medusa; we were alone*
> *I looked you straight in the cold eye, cold.*
> *I was not punished, was not turned to stone.*
> *How to believe the legends I am told?*
>
> *I turned your face around! It is my face.*
> *That frozen rage is what I must explore —*
> *Oh secret, self-enclosed and ravaged place!*
> *That is the gift I thank Medusa for.*[30]

ENDNOTES:

[1] Wolkstein, Diane & Kramer, Samuel. *Inanna, Queen of Heaven and Earth.* Page 12.

[2] Walker, Barbara G. *Woman's Encyclopedia of Myths and Secrets.* Page 629.

[3] Ibid.

[4] Goodrich, Norma Lorre. *Priestesses.*

[5] Harrison, Jane. *Prologomena to the Greek Religion.*

[6] Hamilton, Edith. *Mythology.* New American Library. New York. 1940. Pages 29-30.

[7] Walker. Page 629.

[8] Goodrich. Page 176,

[9] Bulfinch, Thomas. *The Age of Fable.* Page 151.

[10] McLean, Adam. *The Triple Goddess.* Page 39.

[11] Walker. Page 1028.

[12] Goodrich. Page 176.

[13] *Larousse Encyclopedia of Mythology*, Page 203.

[14] Ibid. Page 179.

[15] Ibid. Page 175.

[16] Gimbutas, Maria. *The Civilization of the Goddess.* Page 236.

[17] Ibid.

[18] Ibid.

[19] Ibid.

[20] Numbers, verses 8 and 9.

[21] II Kings, 18:4.

[22] "Cross Cultural Symbolism of the Snake," from *Circle Network News.*

[23] Goodrich. Page 190.

[24] Ibid. Page 188.

[25] Ibid. Page 180.

[26] Ibid. Page 190.

[27] Ibid. Page 191.

[28] Freud, Sigmund. *Collected Papers, Volume 5.* Page 107.

[29] Downing, Christine. *Goddesses—Mythological Images of the Feminine.* Page 111.

[30] Ibid. Page 125.

KALI:

Meeting the Terrible Mother

Invocation to Kali

Kali, Oh Kali Ma,
Dark Mother and Protector,
You go into battle
    wearing a belt of skulls.
You devour demons,
Pierce all illusion,
Beautiful, destroying Mother.

Kali, Oh Kali Ma,
Dark Mother and Protector,
You dance in ecstasy
    celebrating life.
Your breasts full with milk,
Your yoni dripping blood,
Beautiful, destroying Mother,

Kali, Oh Kali Ma,
Dark Mother and Protector,
You sustain the universe
    reflecting perfection.
Your beauty is beyond imagining,
You are terrible and eternal,
Beautiful, destroying Mother.

Root of all bliss.

Kali Ma, is the ancient Hindu goddess, is the archetype of the Mother in its most primitive and powerful form. Kali is a triple goddess of creation, preservation and destruction. Usually spoken of in her destructive phase, Kali is most commonly seen squatting over her dead husband Shiva (Siva), her mouth devouring his entrails while her yoni (vulva) engulfs his lingam (penis). Kali is the hungry sow who devours her young and grows fat on their corpses. She is the image of the terrible mother who is omnipotent and has the power of life and death. Sometimes she is depicted as laying waste to all who cross her path. But as destruction also purifies, so Kali is also considered a creator. She is the warrior goddess, going into battle without fear or ruth; although feminine, she incorporates the principles of aggression, assertion and martial energy. As Kali destroys the old, the new has a chance to be born and grow, initiating another birth, growth and eventual death.

For women to contact Kali, they often have to become violent and terrible—traits not considered feminine nor associated with the "nice little girl" idealization most of us grew up with. Those of us born into middle class families were sheltered and kept away from the violent, wild, bitchy side of woman, unless we had a mother or other female relative who embodied these qualities. Women who had alcoholic mothers or mothers with uncontrollable tempers often encountered this wild, bitchy maenad and became terrified of the "dark mother." Dark skinned women, women with strong African, Semitic, and Asian lineage, as well as women with gypsy blood have often been thought of as portraying Kali Ma. This atavistic projection of equating light skinned, golden haired persons with the "good" and dark skinned, black haired persons with "evil" has caused more grief in society than almost any other illusion.

Kali's Origins

Kali's worship spans the various phases of Indian history from the earliest tribal times. The early Mundan tribes in the Indus and Ganges valleys were Totemists and included blood sacrifice and cannibalism among their practices. The later Dravidians didn't perform blood sacrifices or eat raw meat, but worshipped idols, hanging them with garlands and sprinkling them with sweet incense. The worship of the goddess Kali has carried over from these earlier times into the Brahman and Hindu periods—Kali's bloodthirstiness harking back to the earlier rites of blood sacrifice.[1]

Kali's legend begins when the great goddess Durga (one of Kali's many names) is born from the energies of male divinities who had become impotent after a long, drawn out battle with the demonic forces that dominated the world. All the energies of the male gods united and became one supernova. From the light of that supernova a female Devi (great mother or goddess—the word "divine" comes from the root "devi") was born. This Devi projected overwhelming omnipotence. She had three eyes and was adorned with a crescent moon. Her many arms held weapons and badges, jewels and ornaments, clothing and utensils, garlands and rosaries, all offered by the gods.[2] Her golden body blazed with the splendor of a thousand suns as she sat in her lion or tiger car. Her tremendous force shattered the demon's power.

In one of the great battles destroying the most aggressive man-beasts, Kali sprang forth from the brow of Durga to join in the fierce fighting.[3] Kali thus is known as the "forceful" aspect of Durga.[4] The image of Kali is generally represented as black ("as all colors disappear in black, so all names and forms disappear in her."[5]) In Tantric literature she is described as totally naked, free from all covering of illusion. She is full-breasted; her motherhood is that of giving birth to the cosmos parthenogenetically as she contains the male principle within her.[6]

*Material cause of all change, manifestation, and destruction
...the whole universe rests upon Her, rises out of Her, and
melts away into Her. She is both mother and grave.*[7]

Kali is usually portrayed with a garland of human heads, each representing one of the fifty letters of the Sanskrit alphabet, symbolizing knowledge and wisdom as well as one of the fifty fundamental vibrations in the universe.[8] She wears a girdle of human hands—hands suggest work and karma.[9] Her three eyes indicate past, present, and future. Kali has four hands (or two, six or eight). One left hand holds a severed head, portraying the annihilation of ego-bound evil force, and the other carries the sword of physical extermination with which she cuts the thread of bondage.[10] One right hand gestures to dispel fear and the other exhorts to spiritual strength.[11] "She was cosmic power, the totality of the universe, the harmonization of all opposites, combining wonderfully the terror of absolute destruction with an impersonal, yet motherly, reassurance. Her title is The Ferry Across the Ocean of Existence."[12]

Among the stories about Kali is one concerning her fight with Raktavija, chief warrior of the demons. Seeing that all his soldiers were being killed, Raktavija attacked the goddess himself. She smote him with her weapons, but every drop of blood which fell from his body gave birth to a thousand giants as powerful as he. Kali was only able to overcome him by drinking all his blood. Having conquered him, Kali began to dance with joy so wildly that the whole earth shook. At the request of the gods, her husband begged her to stop but in her madness she did not see him; she cast him down among the dead and trod on his body. Only at last when she realized her mistake did she feel shame.[13]

The Brahmans gave Kali's three functions to three gods: Brahma was the creator; Vishnu, the preserver; and Shiva, the destroyer. But even Vishnu who claimed to have brought the world out of the abyss, honored Kali in a poem, "Material cause of all change, manifestation, and destruction... the whole Universe rests upon Her, rises out of Her, and melts away into Her."[14]

Kali as Shakti Energy

In the Tantric cosmology of India, every entity is seen as a manifestation of Shakti or Shiva, the feminine and masculine principles. Shakti is a "spontaneous vibration;" her blissful state is spoken of in Tantrism as are her joyous outbursts. "When Shakti expands or opens herself, the universe comes into being, and when she gathers or closes herself up, the universe disappears as a manifestation."[15] Shakti is also known as Svatantriya, which means independence or freedom, because her existence does not depend on anything extraneous to herself, and Vimarsa, meaning being many things at the same time.[16] She is regarded as substance because all objects are latent in her womb[17]—they have no existence apart from Shakti. As the embodiment of Shakti, woman is part of the creative principle; she exemplifies the fundamental forces that control the universe. In the Tantric system, the ritual of union is called *asana*; Shakti is represented by a living female who symbolizes the entire female species and, in the ritual, becomes transformed into the flesh and blood of the Goddess.[19] "Innate or acquired personal preferences, youth or age, beauty or ugliness, high or low social status, even relationships, have no significance for the ritual of Shaktism. Indeed, the further the mind is removed from the patriarchal standards of feminine beauty, the better."[20] Any woman can represent the primordial feminine in its purest form as a personification of totality whose essence makes her archetypal.

Male adepts of Shakti energy work through ritual to arouse their own feminine qualities. They often wear the clothes and jewels of women and even observe a few days a month as a period of seclusion.[21]

In Shaktism, the menstrual fluid is sacred; a menstruating woman is connected to the cycles of nature. When a woman bleeds, her feelings go to a center "below the threshold of consciousness"[22] to an intuitive psychic level. In many cultures, a woman is given a special space so she may observe her dreams and visions in solitude and not have to participate in the daily routine of housework, child rearing, and other female chores. This period of seclusion allows her to develop and deepen her intuition. Women who are able to observe their menstrual time as sacred look forward to the monthly flow of blood and do not dread the low energy, headaches and cramping many modern women associate with their monthly cycle.

Menstrual blood is sacred in Tantra and is used for its magical and mystical properties. Today, in Western culture, Women's Blood Mysteries are beginning to be celebrated. For many centuries the Blood Mysteries were a closely guarded secret and practiced only by a few healers, medicine women and witches who kept knowledge of the mysteries alive. In the Tantric practices of India and Tibet, the Blood Mysteries never died. In the group ritual of the left-hand Tantra path, menstrual fluid was often taken as a ritual drink along with wine.[23]

A menstruating woman was often feared because she was thought to have tremendous power and healing capability. In some Native American cultures, a girl who started to menstruate was considered to have exceptional powers. After her puberty ceremony, people were brought to her who needed healing.[24]

The triangle, the *yoni-yantra*, represents the great Mother as the source of life, the cosmic womb. The yoni is considered a sacred area, the gateway to the cosmic mysteries.[25] In many Indian sculptures, the goddess is represented lying on her back with her legs outstretched. Often worshippers kneel between her thighs to drink the *yoni-tattva* or "Sublime Essence."[26] In Kamakhya, India, there is a sacred temple to the Goddess whose shrine is a yoni-shaped cleft in the rock, worshipped as the Yoni of Shakti.

A natural spring within the cave keeps the cleft moist. In July and August, after the first monsoons, an important ceremony takes place. The water runs red with iron oxide and is drunk by the participants as symbolic of menstrual blood.[27] In Kerala there is another ceremony held eight or ten times during the year. At these times a reddened cloth is wrapped around the image of the goddess. The cloth is sought after by visiting pilgrims and prized.[28] Pools of triangular shapes are also considered sacred to the Goddess, and bathing in them is considered auspicious.[29]

In the Yoni-tantra the menstrual fluid is known as the "flower." The Aparajita-flower has a vulvate shape and occupies a specific place in ritual. The lotus (*padma*) is also related to the yoni, and is known as padma-yoni. Brahma, the Creator God in Hinduism, springs from the lotus; in Buddhist symbolism, the lotus represents the yoni.[30] The yoni is likened to the lotus, a symbol of perfection and beauty, in the early stages of its opening as well as in its fully opened form.[31]

Shaktism correlates a woman's monthly cycle with the lunar phases. The body reflects what is happening in the cosmos, and the relationship between a woman's body and the natural cycles is contained in much of Tantric literature. Body language, which is known as the science of Amritakala (kala means fraction), charts the energy centers of the female body according to the calendar of the light and dark halves of the moon.[32] At this time in our history as we go back to the Goddess cultures, we are rediscovering and uncovering many of these earlier practices.

African American women seem to be able to embody the Shakti spirit in Kali, presenting a strong image of both energy and maternalism. Many African American women have been forced by history and social conditions to be both mother and father to their children and to seek to give birth and take care of children outside the bonds of matrimony. This alive, powerful female presence which so many black women possess is the very essence of the Shakti energy. In *Good Woman—Poems and a Memoir, 1969-1980*, Lucille Clifton expressed the Kali archetypal Shakti energy:

> *the coming of Kali*
> *a woman God and terrible*
> *with her skulls and breasts*
> *i am one side of your skin*
> *she sings, softness is the other*
> *you know, you know me well, she sings*
> *you know, you know me well*

running Kali off is hard
she is persistent with her
black terrible self. she
knows places in my bones
i never sing about, but
she knows i know them well
she knows
she knows

Recently, we read a booklet put out by the Women in Trades program at Laney College in Oakland, California. Most of the women in the program were Black, and the booklet was a record of their writings about themselves. All of them were in their early thirties, returning to school to learn a trade and better their education. All had at least one child; many had their first child while in their early or middle teens. Although none of the women were married nor expected to be, all had close family connections with their mothers or other females in the family. None blamed the males for desertion; all expected to assume the burden of raising a child (or children) without a father in the home. All said having their child was the best thing that happened to them; all were proud of being able to return to school to learn a trade. Far from seeing their mothers as "terrible" or intrusive, these women evinced strong bonds of love with the older women in the family— not only their mothers, but grandmothers, aunts and female family friends.

The Name, Kali

From the time Kali first made her entrance in the scriptures (about 400 A.D, in the *Devi Mahatmya*)[33], she has been portrayed as forceful, determined and mightily strong. Ajit Mookerjee tells us that the name "Kali" has been used generically from antiquity to designate the Goddess. She sometimes appears in a frightening form and sometimes in a benevolent one.[34]

In the Sinai, lunar priestesses called themselves Kalu. Priestesses in pre-historic Ireland were Kelles (the origin of the name Kelly). The Sanskrit language from which all Indo-European languages come, was said to have been invented by Kali who created the magic letters of the Sanskrit alphabet and wrote them out on her rosary of skulls. The letters were runes or magic symbols hung around Kali's neck because they stood for primordial creative energy. By creating a word, the world sprang into existence. St. John's "In the beginning was the word," (*logos*) has its origin in the Kali legend.[35]

The Greeks had a world Kalli, meaning beautiful, but they ascribed this "beauty" to objects not normally considered lovely such as demonic centaurs[36]—to things and people that were both beautiful and terrible.

Kali as the Terrible Mother and Dark Goddess was known in Finland as the Black Goddess, Kalma (Kali Ma).[37] Gypsies who originally came from India to the West know her as the Goddess Sara-Kali or St. Sara. Each year modern gypsies make a pilgrimage to a shrine in an ancient cave beneath a cathedral in France. Here there is an image of the Black Madonna known as St. Sara, the Egyptian, an aspect of Kali, the Dark Mother.[38]

Kali as the Beneficent and Terrible Mother

As virgin and creator, Kali is depicted as *sattva-guna*, white; as sustaining mother, *raja*, red; as the absorber of all, *tamas*, black.[39] Kali is an archetype of both birth and death, a giver of life and a destroyer. Kali is most often worshipped today in her form as Dakshinakali, the south- facing black Kali.[40] In this aspect she is usually depicted as standing on the form of Shiva, her husband.[41]

Erich Neumann, in his book, *The Great Mother*, relates that the Terrible Mother is a symbol in the unconscious. She often takes the form of monsters, witches, vampires, and ghouls.[42] The womb of the earth becomes the devouring mother of the underworld, as the woman who generates life takes it back unto herself. Neumann says, "This Terrible Mother is the hungry earth, which devours its own children and fattens on their corpses; it is the tiger and the vulture and the coffin."[43] "It is in India that the experience of the Terrible Mother has been given its most grandiose form as Kali, dark, all-devouring time, the bone-wreathed Lady of the place of skulls."[44] This form of the Goddess is concerned both with the corpses in the underworld as well as the seed corn that is buried beneath the earth.[45] In her aspect as Terrible Mother, Kali raises a skull of "seething blood to her lips."[46] Kali is sometimes depicted squatting among a halo of flames and devouring the entrails of a corpse. She is also shown as standing on the corpse of Shiva, carrying the hacked off heads of her victims.[47] Still another depiction of Kali is one in which she strokes the heads of cobras, with one cobra twined around her waist like a girdle.[48] Here the snake suggests both the aspect of birth, being close to the womb, and the aspect of death. All these diverse aspects are nurturing. When we worship the Mother, we worship her in all her forms.

Just as the Mother in her cosmic aspect destroys, so too, does the Mother in her personal aspect. The very process of bringing up a child implies that the mother must kill some aspects of that child. The good gardener weeds out extra seedlings; so must a good mother weed out unwanted traits in her children. Often this "weeding" kills some part of the child's creativity or spontaneity. The mother who is afraid for her child's safety will curtail her or his adventurous spirit; the mother who is worried about her own image and that of her family will try to mold her child into a person whose behavior is accepted by the community in which they live. Boy children are often sent away from the mother at an early age; the boy child who remains at home "tied to his mother's apron strings" is derided or considered a sissy. On the other hand, the girl child is encouraged to stay at home near her mother and not venture out into the world.

Both sexes fear the power of the mother for she (or a female substitute) had the power of life and death over the once-helpless infant. This power of the mother has been underlined by scientific and psychological writings. Psychology speaks of the "good-enough mother" implying that many mothers aren't good enough and that their children suffer from this lack of goodness.

Women who have problems with their self image pass these problems onto their daughters. Marion Woodman in *Addiction to Perfection* talks about her bulimic and anorexic patients. No matter what their mothers were like, these women seem to have internalized an unpleasant maternal figure. Some had mothers whose idea of femininity was split between the whore and the lady; others had mothers who gave up their own lives for their children's, thus causing their daughters immense guilt, while other mothers repressed their own sexuality. One daughter described her mother as "soft, understanding, intelligent, wants me to be whoever I am—exactly my idea of what a woman should be." If this woman, who idealizes her mother, finds herself talking or dressing like her, she feels she has betrayed her mother for "not fighting to find my own identity as she did."[49] All these women see their mothers as prototypes of the witch, and "witch" does not have a positive connotation for these women.

Woodman also notes that in the Demeter Persephone myth, it was Gaia, the mother of Demeter, who arranged for Hades to capture Persephone, to rape her, remove her from the loving care of her mother, and leave her alone with the male principle in the underworld.[50] She sees this myth as exemplifying the idea that for a woman to grow up, she has to be separated from the mother and carried off by the male rather than taking the natural way to feminine maturity through understanding of her own body. Essentially, ancient and modern female initiation rites are about grounding a girl in her own body, making her comfortable with her own femininity without reference to the male. Puberty rites for young women, as well as working with Kali in ritual, are excellent ways for women to ground their sense of identity in their own bodies.

Frequently we see mothers who rage at their children, punish them harshly, hurt them, and even kill in their anger. This anger is usually at men. Medea is the classical example of female rage which is expressed through her children. Medea was the daughter of King Etes who owned the sheep with golden fleece. King Etes promised Jason the fleece if he or one of his men could harness two fire-breathing bulls and plow a field with them. The task was impossible, but Medea, who had fallen in love at first sight with Jason, gave him a magic ointment with which he could make himself invincible. After Jason, with the aid of the ointment, had successfully plowed the field, Medea went away with him on his ship and protected him through all the trials that befell him on his voyage.

When Jason returned home, he became engaged to the daughter of the King of Corinth. Medea didn't fall for Jason's attempt to rid himself of her for another woman. She had a cloak of precious materials made and gave it to the young princess of Corinth. When the princess tried on the lovely garment, a raging fire enveloped her and melted her body. Then Medea, to complete her revenge, turned on her own children. Knowing she didn't want Jason to have his sons and fearful that, if he took another wife, her children would be treated harshly, she decided:

> I who gave them life, will give them death
> Now no cowardice, no thought of how young they are
> ... I will forget they are my sons
> One moment, one short moment, then forever sorrow.[51]

So Medea, like the archetypal goddess Kali, was able to destroy her young when she was insulted, when she felt justice demanded that her sons be taken away from the man who betrayed her.

Though our society tries to punish those who abuse and kill their children, desperate women are many times not prevented from irrevocably harming their children. We can understand the depths of rage and despair that often lead mothers to abuse and even do away with their children. Many single mothers try to exist in our society without the support of the child's father, and often without the help of an extended family or friends.

These women, left, betrayed, or simply no longer thought of by the men who fathered their children, often take their fear and anger out on their children.

Working with the Goddess Kali

Kali is one of the most frightening goddesses to work with when we seek to express our shadow side. No woman wants to think of herself as the "terrible mother." And it can be very difficult to see one's own mother as terrible. We find comfort in thinking of our mothers as nourishing and protecting; we have been taught to "honor our father and our mother." We feel guilty when we realize that at some time in our past we have hated that frustrating maternal figure deeply. Even if our mother was blatantly neglectful or punitive, we often try to ignore how much we feared, hated or resented her. And if we do feel the hatred and resentment strongly, we certainly do not wish to see that we resemble her in our interaction with our children.

The "terrible mother" is the shadow side of almost all women. Even childless women carry this archetype and try to distance themselves from it. For a mother to recognize that she feels rage towards her child, to act on that rage is truly frightening. Women are expected to be "good-enough mothers." When we call on the goddess Kali, we realize that "goodness" is only one part of the maternal picture. Many women avoid motherhood out of the fear of the "terrible mother" that resides within themselves. Kali's presence can help us come to terms with the angry nurturer within us all.

Another way to work with Kali is to use her to help us express our warrior side. Most women are not brought up to be warriors and do not value the warrior mentality. They do not like war and are quite willing to project the warrior qualities within themselves onto men. Now, however, society is more supportive in allowing women to experience their warrior side. Many women train in self-defense techniques as well as other forms of the martial arts—aikido, judo, karate—to be able to protect themselves and fight back when physically assaulted. Women also are encouraged to become more athletic in general. A female body with well-defined muscles is no longer considered unattractive.

Women are not only fighting back physically, but verbally. At a conference in 1991 called "Women's Voices In Troubling Times" (sponsored by the Women's Alliance and held at the University of California at Berkeley), Dolores Huerta, who helped form the United Farm Workers, spoke of going to Mexico with four men who represented big companies in the U.S. hiring Mexican labor. She went with them to explain how these workers were mistreated and needed certain benefits if they were to continue migrating. Here one woman who spoke out made a difference toward ending a cycle of abuse.

The Anita Hill-Clarence Thomas hearings showed a woman daring to take up the sword and speaking the truth. How the male members of Congress reacted to her is an accurate picture of how far away most American men are from understanding the feelings and sensitivities of women in the workplace. Even though Thomas was eventually nominated to the Supreme Court despite Hill's charges and his own statements of ignorance about women's issues, the case opened the door widely for women to speak up and say, "No." Many other cases of women citing sexual abuse at their jobs followed these hearings.

Kali-Ma, the Dark Mother, holds the two edged sword; she has the power to slay the demons as well as the ability to be compassionate. Sometimes these demons are our own illusions and fantasies about life. Sometimes we are not seeing things for what they really are; we want to live under the illusion that our mates are good providers and love and care for our children; our bosses treat us fairly; our parents understand our ideas and paths in life; our friends respect what we are doing. Or we want to disguise from ourselves our own destructive anger toward people we perceive as helpless, particularly children. For many women, being the victim has become a career; it is more difficult for them to take up their weapons, acknowledge their own anger, and fight for what they want than blame others. At a certain point it becomes necessary to take Kali's sword and cut through the illusions that protect us from seeing and acting on the truth. Doing this is like shedding the snake's skin; we let go of old beliefs and come closer to our own reality. It is not always easy to do this and many go though years of therapy to be able to make significant changes.

Men and Kali

Men, as well as women, naturally fear the "terrible mother." Men who, as children, were pushed out of the nest too early resent the power of the mother and feel abandoned by her. Men who were encouraged to stay too long within the maternal nest and forbidden to bond with their fathers resent maternal influence. While "big mama" is a term of admiration in Black culture, it is one more of fear and dislike in White society. Irvin Yalom in *Love's Executioner* talks frankly about his dislike of fat women. "I have always been repelled by fat women. I find them disgusting; their absurd sidewise waddle, their absence of body contour... and I hate their clothes. How dare they impose that body on the rest of us?"[52] Yalom is a psychiatrist so he tries to probe more deeply into this dislike, "The origins of these sorry feelings? I suppose I could point to the family of fat, controlling women, including—featuring—my mother, who peopled my early life."[53] Yalom does not seem to have similar feelings about fat men; in other words, he doesn't find fat men threatening. It's rather discouraging to think how many therapists who work with women have this negative connection to a woman with an overweight body.

Peter Coyote in *Sleeping Where I Fall* talks of the dislike he feels at looking at women's genitalia. He is turned on by the sight of pubic hair, but says, "I've never understood the pleasure some men derive from 'pink' magazines which feature photos of women posing with their legs spread wide apart spreading their labia with their fingers. Viewed in this way, there is something disquieting and slightly disgusting... the center of birth and disappearance."[54]

With men having such complex and negative reactions to women's bodies, it is no wonder women themselves have trouble accepting their own femininity.

Marcel Proust, who adored his refined and sensitive mother, was possessed on his deathbed by a Kali-like apparition which he described to Celeste, his faithful maid and nurse, "She is so fat and black. She is entirely black. She frightens me. You must not touch her, Celeste, she is implacable, but more and more horrible."[55] Here is the benign personal mother seen as the Kali, death-hag.

Ritual for Working with Kali

It is a good idea to do the Kali ritual, as well as many others in this book, during the Dark Moon phase when there is little light in the sky.

Women should come dressed in saris or any other Indian clothes or ornaments they have, and with any swords or instruments that would be appropriate to Kali-Ma.

The altar could be decorated with skulls and bones, a brazier or incense burner with some joss sticks or other sweet incense, red and black candles, pictures of the Mother in both her benevolent and terrible aspects, and a small bowl with some menstrual blood.

Background music can be sitars or flutes when Kali is invoked. Women can also bring rattles and drums of any kind to use during the ritual.

The High Priestess or four different women invoke Kali through four Hindu goddesses:

In the East we call in Ushas, Goddess of Dawn, to begin this new cycle and help us see through our illusions and seek the truth.

In the South we call in Parvati to bring us the fires of purification so we may be cleansed.

In the West we invoke Durga to teach us to look into the dark places in our beings so that we may not be afraid.

In the North we call in Sarasvati to bring us the wisdom of India, her music and dance, so we may be wise in the traditions of the Goddess.

And now, we call in Kali-Ma, Dark Mother and Goddess, Creatress of all there is.

Before beginning the ritual it is important for the women to discuss which aspect of Kali they want to work with. Trying to increase one's warrior energy is a very different undertaking than attempting to isolate and communicate with the "terrible mother within" oneself. Also, in the spring (perhaps at the new moon when the Sun and the Moon are both in the sign of Taurus), one may do a celebratory ritual honoring life and the Divine Mother, for Kali is the creator as well as the destroyer. A special ritual honoring one's own mother and grandmothers is a beautiful way to honor the loving mother inside each of us.

For a warrior ritual, one woman at a time goes up to the altar and takes an object such as a sword or skull, that exemplifies her interpretation of the warrior energy. With this object, she tells of her need for Kali's energy, her work with bringing forth her aggressive side, and her desire to go forth into the world and slay whatever demons of injustice or oppression burden her. Then she chants and dances out her feelings while the rest of the women drum or play other instruments.

Each woman is encouraged to take her turn. When all the women have finished, the High Priestess dances among the women, blessing them, and putting a drop of menstrual blood on each of them to show that they have been purified through Kali's energy. The women then sit in a circle and discuss ways of being in the world that will encourage their warrior side. If the women meet regularly, there is a chance to discuss working in unison for a cause. Finally, all the women chant and sing to Kali.

Chant—Kali Durga

Kali Durga, Na Mo, Na Mo
Kali Durga, Na Mo, Na Mo[56]
Repeat eight times

Women who are working on enhancing their warrior side would find it helpful to dress in red.

When one works on the "terrible mother", black is the color most conducive to delving deep into one's feelings. In the Kali ritual for the "terrible mother", noises are muted. After calling in the directions, the women can begin to drum softly. At this point, the women all sit down and the High Priestess passes the talking stick. Each woman in the circle takes turns talking about her own mother and the ways in which she felt stifled, neglected and abused as a child. Then, if she has children, she can turn her attention inward to see if she can find some of these traits in herself. Is she like her mother? Or does she, on the other hand, see herself as her mother's opposite? She can share ways in which she resents or is angry with her children or envious of them.

If we share any negative feelings we have toward our own children with other women, we will find Kali grants us an enormous release of guilt. Kali is not a goddess who encourages guilt. She expresses the principle of being aware of one's own feelings and acknowledging them openly. In Kali lies indentification with the birth-giving female, with death and destruction, and with the hope of rebirth. For Kali, all stages of existence are a celebration of life.

Experiences with Kali

Marcia:

Working with Kali has helped me to be stronger and clearer in my actions. When I first connected with Kali's energy, I felt I needed to study Aikido, a martial art that teaches one how to defend oneself, but also shows psychologically where we are vulnerable, where we hedge. After studying Aikido, I became a better driver on the road, more centered and more aggressive. In general, my movements were more defined, both physically and psychologically. My relationships became stronger and cleaner as I learned to be more truthful and not afraid of hurting people's feelings. I visualized myself using Kali's sword to cut through any of my illusions and uncertainties. This technique helped me to come into my own power in a deeper manner.

When I first did the Mother/Grandmother dance, I connected not only with any anger I have had toward my own mother, but also with a deeply compassionate quality. It was interesting to experience both of these feelings at the same time—the terrible and beneficent, the destructive and creative sides. Dancing my Grandmother put me in touch with a whole circle of ancient Grandmothers who hold so much of the wisdom of the planet. They became a source for me to go to whenever I have questions or even when I just want to "hang out" with them and imbibe their wisdom. In a recent interview with Alice Walker, she said that we should have three women elders for president—one Native American, one European American, and one African American. Probably we should include a fourth and fifth as well—an Asian American woman and Latin American.

I also found when doing Kali rituals with a group of women, it has not just been Kali with her wildness and necklace of skulls that the women experienced, but her compassionate side as well.

Gynne:

As do so many women, I grew up perpetually angry at my mother. I can recall sitting on the backstairs as a child and saying to myself over and over, "I'll never do this to *my* children." Then, years later, when I was a mother myself, I'd find myself saying and doing exactly the same things to my own daughter.

I have long wondered why the relationship between mother and daughter in white American culture has been so unpleasant. My own daughter is in a 12-step program. The talk at these meetings and with her friends is almost always on problems in mother-daughter relationships. My perception that her father was emotionally unavailable to her and, at times, downright dishonest with her, seems to be glossed over—perhaps because my daughter blames me for her separation from him in the first place. She probably intuited that I was only a half-hearted mom, part of me wanted to be off working at my own career instead of staying at home with her. Perhaps this conflict in mothers in the the last 20 years has added to the confusion in the daughter's self image—even mom doesn't think it's all right to stay home, do housework, be a mother. It has become necessary to both compete with men and for them.

Working with Kali in ritual and in therapy has made me realize how much I loved my mother and wished to be close to her, although I denied these feelings while she was alive. My mother didn't work, but was an ardent clubwoman, and I resented the time she spent with Hadassah, the PTA and the Sisterhood, although she provided me with a more-than-adequate mother substitute.

I feel a strong mother-daughter relationship is imperative if women are to come into their own power—if they are always battling their mother or the ghost of their mother, they are unable to honor their own femaleness. Kali, who allows one to feel strongly both the positive and negative aspects of the mother, is a way to help women heal the split between their negative and positive self perceptions.

ENDNOTES

[1] Larousse, *Encyclopedia of Mythology*. Page 341.

[2] Mookerjee, Ajit. *Kali The Feminine Force*. Page 49.

[3] Ibid. Page 8.

[4] Ibid.

[5] Mahanirvana Tantra as quoted in Mookerjee. Page 62.

[6] Ibid.

[7] E. A. Rawson as quoted in Walker, Barbara. *Woman's Encyclopedia of Myths & Secrets*. Page 490.

[8] Mookerjee. Page 62.

[9] Ibid.

[10] Ibid.

[11] Ibid.

[12] Ibid.

[13] Larousse. *Encyclopedia of Mythology*. Page 350.

[14] E. A. Rawson as quoted in Walker. Page 490.

[15] Mookerjee. Page 23 from *Spanda Karikas The Divine Pulsation*, translated by Jaidea Singh.

[16] Ibid. Page 23.

[17] Ibid.

[18] Garrison. *Tantra: the Yoga of Sex*. Page 11.

[19] Mookerjee. Page 25.

[20] Ibid.

[21] Ibid. Page 26.

[22] Ibid. Pages 32-33.

[23] Ibid.

[24] Niethammer, Carolyn. *Daughters of the Earth*. Page 39.

[25] Mookerjee. Page 30.

[26] Ibid.

[27] Ibid.

[28] Ibid. Page 31.

[29] Ibid.

[30] Ibid.

[31] Ibid. Page 35.

[32] Ibid.

[33] Ibid.

[34] Ibid.

[35] Walker. Page 491.

[36] Ibid. Page 492.

[37] Mookerjee. Page 72.

[38] Katlyn, "Goddess of the Gypsies" in Sage Woman magazine, vol.III, #11.

[39] Ibid. Page 62.

[40] Mookerjee. Page 62.

[41] Ibid. Page 63.

[42] Neumann, Erich. *The Great Mother*. Page 149.

[43] Ibid.

[44] Ibid. Page 150.

[45] Ibid. Page 151.

[46] Ibid. Page 152.

[47] Ibid. Page 153.

[48] Ibid.

[49] Woodman, Marion. *Addiction to Perfection*. Page 120.

[50] Ibid.

[51] Hamilton, Edith. *Mythology*. Page 130.

[52] Yalom, Irvin D. *Love's Executioner & Other Tales of Psychotherapy*. Pages 87-88.

[53] Ibid.

[54] Coyote, Peter in *Roots and Branches: Contemporary Essays by West Coast Writers*. Page 224.

[55] Miller, Milton L. MD. *Nostalgia, A Psychoanalytic Study of Marcel Proust*. Page 23.

[56] from the tape, *Songs to the Divine Mother, Jai Ma Kirtan*

SEHKMET:

Escaping From Feelings

Inovocation to Sekhmet

Before
the beginning
When there was everything
When there was nothing
When out of the void
came matter
When man and animal were one
When the Goddess had no face
When a lioness was the face of the Goddess

Lady of the beginning
Beautiful inhuman eye
Giving life to two lands
Self contained
She who is the source
She who is the mother of images

Out of the great silence
Roamer of the desert
Destroyer of appearances
Devourer and creator
She who is
and is not

Beloved Sekhmet

W ith Sekhmet we go far back to a time when the goddesses and gods were scarcely human or even animal. Often representations of early deities look like the rock from which they were carved. Even if their features were once present and have been erased by time, the blank, monolithic forms of some of the earlier goddesses seem to evoke a period when humans first began to try to reach away from the physical, upward to the unknown and the spiritual. Their haunting, almost featureless faces evoke the mystery of the Great Beginning.

Sekhmet is usually depicted with a lioness's head and a woman's body, sitting on a throne, her hands placed palms down on her knees with an ankh in her right hand. She has some 4000 names which describe her various aspects and attributes. One name was known only to Sekhmet and eight associated deities; and one name (known only to Sekhmet herself) was the means by which Sekhmet could modify her being or cease to exist. The possibility of "not to be, of returning to nothingness, distinguishes goddesses and gods of Egypt from deities of all other pantheons."[1]

It may seem strange to include Sekhmet in a book dealing with the dark goddesses since she is so obviously a Solar rather than a Lunar goddess. This is part of the paradox of Sekhmet. She is a Solar goddess who lives in the hot desert, has the face of a lioness (later connected with the astrological sign Leo), and yet she contains aspects that are considered dark or, at least, unpleasant and usually found in only the Lunar goddesses. She is ecstatic, passionate, protective of the souls of the dead in the underworld, can be full of wrath, is a fearless and pitiless warrior, and is associated with menstrual blood.

Sekhmet and Her Family

Sekhmet is among the most ancient of the early Egyptian deities. She was the wife and sister of the god Ptah, and the mother of Nefer-Tem. Ptah's name means opener; in fact, Ptah was thought to be the opener of the day just as Tem was the closer. E. A. Wallis Budge, the great Egyptologist, thinks "opener" in the case of Ptah has the meaning of engraving or carving with a chisel.[2] At a very early period Ptah was identified as one of the great primeval gods of Egypt and called "the very great god who came into being at the earliest time."[3] He is usually shown as a mummified figure with only his arms and hands free. His specialty is smelting and building, and one of his titles is "master builder." He is also believed to shape the new bodies in which the souls of the dead reside when they go to live in the underworld.[4]

According to the Larousse *Encyclopodia of Mythology*, Sekhmet is another name for Hathor, an Egyptian goddess whom the Greeks identify with Aphrodite. Hathor was both the wife and daughter of Ra, the sun god. She represents what is true, good, and beautiful—all that is "best in wife, mother, and daughter."[5] Aphrodite was married to Hephaestos (or Vulcan), the lame forger of the Greek gods; Sekhmet was married to Ptah, a god who works in metal and stone and is usually depicted as severely physically restricted. Like Aphrodite, Sekhmet, under one of her many aspects, is considered a goddess of powerful sexual passions and is one of the figures Christians mean when they refer to the Whore of Babylon or the "red hag."

Sekhmet and Ptah had a son, Nefer-Tem, who gave medicine to humans and had the ability to transform himself into the lotus flower. A later form of Nefer-Tem is the Greek Asclepius, known as the father of medicine. In her role as Nefer-Tem's mother, Sekhmet was called The Great One of Healing. Her priests were the greatest of healers and Nefer-Tem was the God of physicians.[6]

Sekhmet is one of the most ancient deities known to the human race—much older than her husband/brother Ptah.[7] Sekhmet's father is Ra, the sun god—the king of the Egyptian gods. She was considered the "Eye of Ra" and was placed as the uraeus (serpent) on Ra's brow where she guarded the sun god's head and spat forth flames at his enemies.[8] She came to Egypt from a "place unknown and at a time unrecorded."[9] Her name, Lady of the Flame, refers to her mastery over the sun's power.

One of Sekhmet's sisters is Bast, who had the body of a woman and the head of a cat. Her cult is the reason the cat is sacred in Egypt. Bast had a very different character from Sekhmet's. Although the cat was honored for its strength, virility and agility, Bast was considered a kindly goddess representing the beneficent powers of the sun protecting Egypt. Her color is green for the sun's gift of the budding grain in the spring. Sometimes she was considered a Moon goddess. She was also known as the goddess of joy —her cult was celebrated in lighthearted barge processions and orgiastic ceremonies.[10]

Sekhmet could be considered the Shadow side of Bast. The seeming anomaly that Bast was a Lunar goddess and Sekhmet always a Solar one is not so mysterious when you consider that the Egyptians, more than any other near-Eastern peoples, were able to incorporate both the feminine and masculine in their pantheon, with no tendency to malign or denigrate either energy.

But truly, Sekhmet has no shadow side. Since she comes from a time when deities were considered half animal, half human, she has the quality of the animal which is to be fully itself and not split as human consciousness is. No stories about Sekhmet express her feeling horror at any of her actions, however bloodthirsty, or about any of her attributes, however unpleasant. Later worshippers split Sekhmet into different goddessess—some of these considered evil, others good.

The Story of Sekhmet

Sekhmet means strong or powerful. She is the personification of fierce, scorching and destroying heat. A passage from the *Book of the Dead* reads:

> *Lady of the red apparel...sovereign of her father, superior*
> *to whom the gods cannot be...thou who are pre-eminent, who*
> *riseth in the seat of silence...who is mightier than the gods*
> *...who art the source, the mother, from whence souls come and*
> *who makest a place for them in the hidden underworld...and the*
> *abode of everlastingness.*[11]

As the above quote indicates, Sekhmet is another form of the triple goddess who presides over birth, life, and death.

In the most famous story told about Sekhmet, humans conspired to overthrow the gods. They swore great oaths against Ra and plotted the downfall of all the gods by using the same powers the gods had given to men. Ra got word of this plot, and, after taking counsel amongst the other gods, decided that Sekhmet, the "force against which no other force avails" should appear on earth and quash the rebellion.

Once given these instructions, Sekhmet's fury knew no end. She went down to earth, and, night after night, walked among humankind, slaughtering, tearing and rending bodies; wading in and drinking human blood. Nothing could stop the carnage for Sekhmet was intoxicated on human blood.

Finally, the gods realized that Sekhmet would continue on her bloody way until the last human had been killed. Ra caused a powerful, mind altering drug to be brewed, and sent the mixture to the god Sekti. Sekti added beer and human blood to the potion and made 7000 jars of the mixture. These jars were taken to a place where Sekhmet would pass and the contents poured out on the ground. When Sekhmet arrived and saw what she took to be human blood, she lapped up all the liquid. After drinking, her heart became filled with joy; she was content and had no further desire to continue destroying humans.

Although Sekhmet is ferocious, her powers were used protectively. A goddess of wrath, she reacts with total savagery whenever she or her allies are attacked or wronged, but there is no evidence of her provoking conflict.[12]

Sekhmet contains within herself the powerful energy called Kundalini in the Tantric tradition. As does Kali, she represents Shakti which unites psychic and cosmic energy. Because of this, she is called the "lady of the scarlet-colored garment" and known for her sexual prowess.

The Meaning of Sekhmet

Sekhmet has much in common with many of the dark goddesses we have already discussed. Like Lillith she has the reputation of being sexually free and of residing in the desert in a state of wildness—even to the extent that she is seen as half beast, half human. Along with Kali, she is capable of unbridled destructiveness and is an avatar of Shakti or cosmic energy. The red halo that surrounds her and the story of her drinking human blood again parallel the associations of the dark goddesses with menstrual blood.

Sekhmet is older than any other of the goddesses we have discussed, indicating that the concept of the triple goddess who controls the fate of humankind—birth, life, death—is as old as human history itself. She, indeed, comes from the time when "god was a woman."

Although Sekhmet is described as all-powerful, terrifying and the "force against which no other force avails," she is susceptible to trickery. In order to deter her from her purpose, the gods made her drunk. In this way, Sekhmet represents the shadow side of woman who allows herself to be deflected from her anger and her purpose by love, alcohol, cigarettes, food, drugs or any other addictive substance.

Not so long ago, it was common to have women "put away." Often these women were ones who were "acting out" sexually, who demanded power or the right to learn or do something usually reserved only for men, or who had wealth of their own that was coveted by members of their family or by the state. Since the male of the family had most of the rights, it was easy for a father, husband or brother to have an obstreperous female family member incarcerated. Often, all that was needed was for a woman to be told she was "ill." Then she could retire to her room and "quack" herself, as female medicine-taking used to be called derisively. Today, women are the greatest customers of mood-altering or calming drugs and the preponderance of therapy patients are women. The theory is always that there is nothing wrong with society or with men; it is the woman who is acting unreasonably and needs to be restrained. Of course, men too are subject to addictions. As Freud indicated, civilization is difficult for humans; many sacrifices have to be made in order to attain the repression necessary for living in civilized societies. Unfortunately, what is repressed and not acknowledged comes out destructively in other ways.

When we talk of working with the shadow side, we are talking about unconscious beliefs people hold about themselves. Many women feel they are "nervous" and need sedatives, or worry that they might be destructive or get out of hand and need therapy or help. The "terrible mother" often worries that she will be destructive to her children and drinks or takes pills so she can present a reasonable front to her family. Of course, if she drinks too much, she then is a candidate for another kind of rehabilitation and considered a social pariah as well. Drugs, alcohol and cigarettes help conceal not only rage, but also depression. We personally know of two women, both long-time smokers, who cried frequently and uncontrollably for many months after they quit. Only when they quit smoking did they learn about the excess of sorrow they had buried beneath this habit.

Other women's addictive patterns are more subtle and may not involve substance abuse. Some women turn on the television as soon as they begin to get depressed or are uncomfortable with the feelings surfacing in themselves. Television, video tapes and books can all work to sedate the emotions. Attracting abusive and dysfunctional relationships is a way of not confronting feelings; blaming others for their inadequacies is another type of addictive pattern. Clarissa Pinkola Estes makes this comparison in *Women Who Run With the Wolves*. She says that drugs and alcohol are very much like an abusive lover who treats you well, then beats you up, apologizes, and does it again.

Blaming others individually or in groups is something that we all do as a way of not confronting our own emotions. Through most of this book, we have tried to avoid using the term "patriarchy" because in women's literature the patriarchy has become the standard scapegoat of any and all ills suffered by the female sex. With the dark goddesses, we are not focusing on women as victims. It is important for women to realize that "patriarchy" is a mode of consciousness and has nothing to do with gender. Patriarchy refers to "power over" others or things; it also connotes a linear way of thinking—inflexible and totally lacking compassion and understanding. To condemn civilization because it is necessarily repressive and has largely been ruled by men is self-defeating. Instead, women need to take charge of their own lives (as more of them are) and responsibility for the condition of the planet. From responsibility, which is an active condition and not one of sedation, change occurs.

Sexual addictions are becoming more prevalent in our society. Addictive sex occurs any time a woman uses sex to express anger or feel powerful, or needs to relieve tension, hide from feelings, or create a false bond of intimacy. Addiction occurs when a woman feels increasingly unable to control her behavior. Addictive sex usually leads to harmful consequences, obsessions, and a decreased ability to function. "Sex addiction in women reflects an internalization of male norms of sexuality involving power, aggressiveness, and control."[13] Co-dependent sexual behavior, which is not as aggressive, is even more common among women and more acceptable, but just as harmful. Here women become addicted to abusive or unsatisfactory partners in a way that inhibits their functioning in other areas of their lives.

Anorexia and bulimia have been described as "ritual" addictions by Jungian analyst Marion Woodman in *Addiction to Perfection*. Both anorexics and bulimics engage in ritual behavior and carry out these rituals alone. Addiction itself, can be considered ritualistic behavior. Woodman thinks the prevalence of addictions has something to do with the failure of organized religion to provide meaningful rituals for contemporary persons. That is one reason why Alcoholics Anonymous, Overeaters Anonymous, Narcotics Anonymous and all the other 12-step programs, by stressing ritualized behavior and following a definite ritual at their meetings, have such success in helping people control their behaviors. She also thinks eating disorders are related to the "terrible mother."

Women who worry that they may "get out of control," who have a difficult time facing the everyday demands or routine of their lives, who feel they have sacrificed themselves to their husbands, lovers or children, or feel still in the grip of the "terrible mother," can work with Sekhmet (and Kali) in ritual.

The goddess Sekhmet, to protect her father and her brother gods, ran amok. Once started, she developed a taste for blood and couldn't stop until she was tricked into imbibing a strong narcotic disguised as human blood. While it probably was a wise decision of Ra's not to allow Sekhmet to continue wantonly killing all of humanity, the practice of giving the "wild woman" narcotics to calm her and control her behavior is a common one in modern society and one that has much less justification. What does this tale have to do with the shadow many women carry? It clearly illustrates how women, already taught to fear their own power, are further subverted by society which offers all kinds of placebos and distractions, while, on the other hand, condemning the female alcoholic or drug user.

Ritual for Invoking Sekhmet

Women should come to this ritual dressed in shades of red, orange, and yellow (to represent the solar energy which Sekhmet stands for) and wearing animal masks. The ritual should occur outdoors, if possible, and in as wild an environment as possible. An interesting way to perform this ritual is in the hot sun, as the heat of the sun brings out the energy of Sekhmet who lives in the hot desert. There should be plenty of space to allow women to move freely and to make animal noises as they connect with their deep animal nature. A small fire in a cauldron or fire pit will help provide heat and may be used for the burning of the papers at the end of the ritual.

The altar may be decorated with statues of Sekhmet, animal bones, bird feathers, red candles and a cauldron of some red colored liquid symbolizing human blood.

When all the women are smudged and the circle has been cast, the High Priestess or leader calls in the four directions:

To the East we call in Bast, Goddess of the Green Oasis, who brings beauty and compassion to the world.

To the South we call in Nekhebet, Vulture Goddess of the South, who sees far and clearly and burns a path through falseness and deceit.

To the West we call in Sekhmet, Goddess of the Setting Sun and Queen of the Libyan Desert, who protects the dead in the underworld.

To the North we call in Uatchet, Snake Goddess of the North, who gives to humans wisdom and protection from evil.

(Bast, Nekhebet, and Uatchet are all aspects or sisters of Sekhmet.)

Women drum and rattle to bring in the energy of Sekhmet. Some of them begin to move in imitation of their animal selves. Then, one by one, each woman dances out her animal, cleansing herself of guilt, remorse, worry, and fear about or for others. After the dances, each woman takes a cup of the red liquid, sips it and pours it on the ground. She shares with the others how she will bring passion into her life and vows to give up any addictions or addictive habits (for a short time at least) which keep her from connecting with her deeper animal nature.

After each woman talks, the group agrees to meet after a specified time period to discuss the results of their abstention and the difficulties they encountered, as well as any transformations that have occurred.

At the end of the ritual, each woman writes on a piece of paper at least one addiction or habit she wishes to give up; she then burns the paper in the fire. All drink some purified water and dance in celebration, taking into their bodies the strong Sekhmet energy, while some beat drums to continue to call up Sekhmet's spirit.

After the circle is closed and the directions thanked, the women may feast on sensual red foods or any Egyptian or Middle Eastern dishes.

The purpose of the Sekhmet ritual is to allow women to experience and become aware of all the parts of their lives that inhibit or sedate the strong expression of feeling or passion. Naturally, one cannot live as Sekhmet all the time, but one can realize *through experience* exactly how many feelings are repressed in the name of conformity as well as the desire to please and get along.

Personal Experiences in Ritual with Sekhmet

Marcia:

My strongest experiences with Sekhmet have occurred in the high deserts of New Mexico and Arizona. One feels the heat of the sun here in a much more intense way. Nature is more dramatic with its thunderstorms and lightning, making it easier to access one's passions. When I spend time in the desert, I try not to bring reading material to engage my mind, and try also not to write too much even though writing is for me an easy way of expressing myself. Instead, I have learned to let my feelings speak through my drum and my rattle. The most incredible experiences of drumming I have ever had occurred in the Southwest (perhaps that is one of the reasons

I am moving to New Mexico). It is as though the drum spoke through me, took over my body and was playing me rather than I playing it. It spoke with such passion that I was literally "gone" for a while, meaning my mind was gone, which is never easy. Astrologically, I have a Gemini Moon opposite the planet Mercury, and my mind is constantly working on all sorts of details. Not to read and not to write are good exercises for me. To allow myself to feel and become one with the environment— the birds and the animals—has not always been easy, but is deeply pleasurable. I see that I can anaesthetize myself with mental data and configurations which is another kind of pleasure (I am also an astrologer) as long as I balance my diet and get away to the desert or woods backpacking or doing small vision quests.

Gynne:

Sekhmet to me is the oldest and most mysterious goddess I have worked with. Her life in the desert and her fierce warrior-like nature is entirely unfamiliar to me. I do not like heat, and I am a city person. As a child I totally understood why St. Augustine called his work *The City of God* (where else would God live, but in a city?) and why Samuel Johnson said, "When a man is tired of London, he is tired of life." So working with Sekhmet means radically changing my consciousness.

Before I do any ritual, I like to prepare myself. I usually try to do a chakra meditation at home to open up and feel each chakra. (I really like Vicki Noble's tape on working with the chakras based on her *Motherpeace Tarot*.) With Sekhmet, I particularly want to open and explore the root chakra and the third chakra dealing with assertion. Then, when I come to the ritual, I am open to the Sekhmet energy.

I like this quote from Marion Woodman. "Ritual is recognized as a transformative fire through which an individual moves on the journey from one level of society to another or from one level of awareness to another. Whether the fire is real or symbolic, the initiate submits to it, allows the old life to be burned away, and emerges a new person. At the center of the fire is an archetypal force, a god or goddess, which the participant invokes in order to participate in its life. By contacting that energy in a numinous experience... the ego... is enlarged and transformed so that it returns to ordinary life with a new outlook."[14]

ENDNOTES:

[1] Masters, Robert. *The Goddess Sekhmet*. Llewellyn, St. Paul Minn. 1991. Page 54.

[2] Budge, E. A. Wallis. *The Gods of the Egyptians*, Vol I. Dover Books, New York. Page 500.

[3] Ibid. Page 501.

[4] Ibid.

[5] Ibid. Page 435.

[6] Masters. Page 48.

[7] Ibid. Page 44.

[8] Patrick, Richard. *Color Book of Egypt*. Page 42.

[9] Ibid. p. 44.

[10] Ions, Veronica. *Egyptian Mythology*. Page 103.

[11] Patrick. Page 45.

[12] Ibid. Page 48.

[13] Kasl, Charlotte Davis. *Women, Sex, and Addiction*. Page 43.

[14] Woodman, Marion. *Addiction to Perfection*. Page 31.

HECATE:

Accepting Dissolution and Change

Invocation to Hecate

Hecate,
Mistress of the Dark Moon
standing at the crossroads
with howling hounds
and blazing torches.

Dark Crone Mother
you light our way
with dreams and prophecies
you guide us
through visions and magic.

In the depths of the underground
we find you
and your priestesses
chanting funerary hymns
and incantations.

Beside the sacred poplar and yew,
we feel your presence
as we move from the darkness
of our unconscious sleep
and are awakened to change
by your call.

Hecate is an ancient goddess from an early, pre-Greek period of myth. At first the Hellenic Greeks found Hecate difficult to fit into their pantheon. Although she was not considered a part of the Olympian company, she had retained dominion over sky, earth, and underworld, making her the bestower of wealth and the blessings of life. Zeus himself honored Hecate so greatly that he always conceded to her the ancient power of giving or denying to mortals any desired gift. Later, during the Middle Ages, Hecate became associated with black magic and was debased as the hag, or Queen of the Witches, who led Satanic rites.

Hecate is skilled in the arts of divining and foretelling the future. She gives humans dreams and visions which, if interpreted wisely, lead to greater clarity. Also, because of her association with Persephone, she is connected to death and regeneration. Her presence in the land of the underworld allows for the pre-Hellenic hope of re-birth and transformation, as opposed to Hades, who represented the inevitability of death.

Hecate's Origins and Genealogy

Hecate's name derives from the Egyptian midwife-goddess Heqit, Hekct, or Hekat. The heq was the tribal matriarch of pre-dynastic Egypt and was known as a wise woman.[1] Heket was a frog headed Goddess who was connected with the embryonic state when dead grain decomposed and began to germinate. She was also one of the midwives who assisted every morning at the birth of the Sun.[2]

In Greece, Hecate was a Moon Goddess, one of the original trinity who were connected with the Moon's three phases and ruled heaven, earth and the underworld. She was especially worshipped at places where three roads met and was known as Hecate Trevia, Hecate of the Three Ways.[3] At these places the Greeks erected three-faced statues called Hecataea and left offerings of ritual food especially on the Full Moon; travelers sacrificed to Hecate to protect them on their journeys.[4]

Hesiod in *Theogony* says that Hecate was the daughter of the Titan Perses and the Titaness Asteria, a star goddess, both symbols of shining light. Asteria was a sister of Leto who gave birth to Apollo and Artemis, making Hecate a cousin to Artemis.[5] An even older tradition saw her as a more primal goddess and made her a daughter of Erebus and Nyx (night). From the union between Night and Erebus sprang Doom, Old Age, Death, Murder, Continence, Sleep, Dreams, Discord, Misery, Vexation, Nemesis, Joy, Friendship, Pity, the three Fates, and the three Hesperides (daughters of the Sunset whose realm lies in the far west).[6] If we look carefully at the various children of this union, we can see almost all of the attributes given to Hecate at one time or another.

A later tradition says Hecate was the daughter of Zeus and Hera. She apparently angered Hera by stealing her rouge to give to Europa. After doing this, she hid in the house of a woman who had just given birth; this contact made Hecate impure. To remove her stain, the Cabeiri (servants of Persephone, who save sailors from shipwreck) plunged her into the river Acheron, which carried her underground where she married Hades.[7]

In the underworld, Hecate was known as Prytania, Queen of the Dead. She was in charge of expiations and also sent demons to earth to torment humankind.[8] She herself appeared with her dogs at crossroads, at tombs (like Kali), and at scenes of crimes.

Connecting Hecate with childbirth stems from her origin as Heket, but it was the later Hellenic myth that made Hecate "impure" from the blood of childbirth and caused her to be plunged into the river Acheron. Like so many of the Dark Goddesses, Hecate has an association with menstrual blood, originally considered holy and mysterious, but later thought of as unclean. Barbara Walker says that this is an old myth "derived from patriarchal anxieties" about contact with childbearing women, demonstrated in the Bible especially (Leviticus 12:5).[9]

During the Middle Ages, Hecate became known as Queen of the Witches. Catholic authorities said that the people most dangerous to the faith were those whom Hecate patronized—midwives, healers, and seers.[10] They also saw the simple peasants practicing folk religion as "devil worshippers," and Hecate was portrayed as an ugly hag leading covens of witches in these practices.[11] In the name of purifying the church and the body of Christ, nine million witches, mostly women, were burned and tortured, a crime that has never been fully discussed in the annals of Western history.

Hecate's Triple Nature

Hecate represents many forms of the triple goddess. As Moon Goddess, Hecate is the dark face of the Moon, while Artemis represented the New Moon, and Selene, the Full Moon. These three goddesses also symbolized heaven (Selene), earth (Artemis, the huntress), and the underworld (Hecate). Hecate also conforms to the Crone phase of the triple goddess in the trio with Persephone or Kore (the maiden), and Ceres, the mother. These three phases were often seen as one being with three faces. In women's agricultural mysteries, her trinity took form as Kore, the green corn; Persephone, the ripe ear; and Hecate, the harvested corn.[12]

Hecate was often shown with three heads—lion, dog and mare (later depicted as dog, snake, and lion according to some accounts), the dog being the Dog-star Sirius.[13] She is also shown in the form of a pillar, the Hectaerion, with three heads and six arms bearing three torches and three sacred symbols: a key for her role as guardian of the ancient mysteries of the underworld, a rope or scourge for her role of bringing souls into the underworld and helping them to be reborn, and a dagger. The dagger later became the *athame* of the witches, which is related to the sword that cuts through delusion and is a symbol of ritual power.[14]

Hecate's animal companion was the three headed dog Cerberus, who was once fifty-headed, but eventually became three-headed like his mistress.[15] Cerberus was the Greek counterpart of Anubis, the dog-headed son of the Libyan Death goddess Nephthys, who conducted souls to the underworld.[16]

This three-fold nature of the Goddess was used by the early Catholic church in its teachings of the Father, Son, and Holy Ghost—who are analogous to the Maiden, Mother, and Crone—the Crone's property of wisdom going to the Holy Ghost or Spirit. The Holy Spirit, through appearing to the apostles at Pentecost, imparted wisdom of spiritual matters to Christ's disciples so they could go forth and spread the word of God from which sprang the Holy Church. The Holy Spirit is considered by Catholics the breath between Christ and God. Like Hecate, the Holy Spirit is related to "speaking in tongues" and the gift of prophecy. The ancient "mother" wisdom of Hecate is disembodied in the Holy Spirit, but the connection to inspiration and knowledge beyond the ken of ordinary people remains.

Another parallel between Christianity and the triple goddess are the three Maries who appear at the tomb of the resurrection as Mary, the Virgin; Mary of Bethany, wife of Cleopas; and Mary Magdalene.[17] Recent research has brought forth the role of the Magdalene as the archetype of the High

Priestess, wise woman, Crone. (See Clysta Kinstler's novel, *The Moon Under Her Feet*, for a fictionalized account) and the writings of Elizabeth Van Buren, such as *Refuge of the Apocalypse*, which discusses the Magdalene's flight into Southern France, where many sanctuaries and holy places dedicated to her are still extant.) Shrines to the Black Madonna have been uncovered and catalogued throughout Europe, bearing witness to this third aspect of the Virgin Mary.

Hecate as Prytania, Queen of the Dead

One of Hecate's main associations is as Queen of the underworld. She lived underground along with Hades and other underworld deities. Hecate was the only person to hear Persephone's screams as she was carried down to the underworld, and it was Hecate who informed Demeter of the fate of her daughter. She also guided Persephone in her ascent back to the upper world (symbolic of the re-birth of the soul, which occurs at the winter solstice).[18] Persephone, who is faithful to Hades, but has no children by him, prefers the company of Hecate to his.

In the underworld, after newly-arrived ghosts are met and judged by Minos, Rhadamanthys, and Aeacus at the place where three roads meet, Hecate then directs souls to the correct road for the particular realm to which they were assigned—Tartarus, a walled place of punishment is designed for the enemies of the Gods; the Asphodel Meadows is for the person who is neither evil nor good; and the fields of Elysium are orchards under which the virtuous can enjoy perennial soft breezes. Hecate was in charge of the regeneration or transformation of souls that came into the underworld. She was a guardian and teacher instructing souls in occult and magical rites, preparing them for the next step of their journey, reincarnation.

Hecate also has been portrayed with her pack of black, baying hounds visiting the graves of the dead and searching for souls to carry into the underworld.Sometimes, Hecate herself was addressed as a "black she-dog."[19] Dogs howling at the moon are seen as harbingers of death.

The Erinnyes or Furies also accompanied Hecate on occasion. The Erinnyes personified the pangs of conscience that come from breaking a taboo. They avenged the spilling of blood, particularly the murder of a parent, and more particularly the murder of a mother, since the first taboo was the disobedience, insult, or violence to the mother.[20] The Erinnyes later became the Eumenides (or kind ones), softening their nature and moving their acts away from the avenging of mother-right. The third play of the

Oresteia, which we discussed earlier in the chapter on Medusa, depicts how Orestes was tried and acquitted by Athena, who was "always for the father". Before his acquittal, the Erinnyes followed him implacably for the murder of his mother, Clytemnestra.

Black poplars and yew trees were sacred to Hecate as death goddess. White poplars were sacred to Persephone because white suggests rebirth or resurrection.[21] Yew trees take the longest to mature of any trees, aside from oaks. Oaks were special to the Druids and other groups who worked with the mysteries of death and regeneration.

This regenerative quality of Hecate's, her ability to bring about change, is one we celebrate each year on All Hallows. Although Halloween is one of the festivals deriving from the Celtic tradition, the similarities between Cerridwyn (Welsh triple goddess whose cult goes back to the pre-historic temples of ancient Malta) and Hecate are many. The use of the cauldron, the ability to see beyond the veil to those who have gone to the other side, and the commemoration of the year's end and the death of the old year, are all qualities of this holiday which is a cross-quarter day (halfway between the Fall Equinox and Winter Solstice) and one of the eight Sabbats universally celebrated by witches.

Hecate as Seer, Prophet and Visionary

Hecate is known for her gifts of prophecy, her clear vision and her knowledge of the magical and occult arts. Because she stands at the crossroads, she can look into the past, present and future. Her priestesses were many, including Medea and Circe. Medea had Hecate's foresight and wisdom; Circe her gift of the magical arts. Since Hecate had three faces, she could look to the past, the present and the future; thus she was highly skilled as a visionary.

Hecate's worshippers invoked her in ritual and placed food for her as an offering. This was known as Hecate's suppers. Rituals were always in the darkest hours of the night. Worshippers gathered to study and learn occult wisdom (later referred to as the "black arts"). Initiations in the name of Hecate are still carried on by many witches and certain covens. Initiates are taught the arts of scrying (reading from a crystal ball), astrology, Tarot, numerology, and the making of herbal medicines and incenses. All of these arts are ways of accessing esoteric knowledge and gaining a greater understanding the mysteries of the psyche. They are all empowering insofar as they provide us with maps and keys to our individual plans and purposes on earth.

Since Medieval times and the burning of the wise women (witches), these magical arts have stayed underground and are called the "occult arts." The study of astrology and numerology is basic to our understanding of everyday life and ideally should be taught as a part of the school curriculum as they were in ancient times. The knowledge of herbalism and making medicine from natural plants and substances has been resurrected in our time, though not without much controversy from the established medical hierarchy. Understanding the special healing properties of plants and herbs should be a part of every doctor's training.

Hecate and Other Dark Goddesses

There are many themes common among the Dark Goddesses of different cultures. We have seen how descriptions of Hecate at tombs and graveyards are similar to those of Kali. Kali is pictured with many arms and several heads; Hecate has three faces and is sometimes shown with six arms carrying torches.

In the Greek mythology, the Empusae were said to be the children of Hecate. The Empusae are demons that are "ass-haunched and wear brazen (bronze) slippers." They disguise themselves as bitches, cows, or beautiful maidens; and as maidens, lie with men at night sucking their vital forces.[22] Graves suggests that this concept may have been brought to Greece from Palestine, where they went by the name of Lilim (children of Lilith). Hecate supposedly wore a bronze sandal as opposed to Aphrodite who wore a golden one, and her daughters, the Empusae, followed her example.[23] Certainly similarity can be seen between Hecate and the Empusae with Lilith who was said to suck the vitality of men through sexual intercourse which she initiated in a stealthy manner. It is interesting that Hecate can be compared with Lilith because their attributes, except for begetting evil children, are very different.

The caverns of the underworld and the description of the realm of Tartarus remind us of Ereshkigal and the filthy hell in which she resided, although Hecate had far more power of action than Ereshkigal and was not left alone below ground.

Hecate and the Shadow Side

Working with Hecate is a way to access our intuitive and inspired side. Intuition and "knowing" is a gift that many have hidden and feared. When gifted with prophetic vision, some people have felt they were going mad, touching the fringes of lunacy from which they would never return (much like the shamanic journey into another realm through the taking of a psychedelic plant). Because second-sight and prophecy have been called "irrational," having this gift can be very frightening since it is possible to lose touch with ordinary, earth reality. Also, people who claim to have visions are derided and even locked up by others. Perhaps that is why we need good teachers to transmit the idea that the wisdom of Hecate is a wisdom beyond common sense and can be used for healing and creativity. It is certainly empowering to understand the workings of the universe or the psyche, whether this knowledge comes from scientific study or an intuitive grasping of the structure of nature.

Because female nature is related to the moon, women often rely more on experience and intuition, while men tend more toward using logic and rational thinking, which operate in a Solar manner. Both modes of consciousness, the Lunar and Solar, should be balanced. Unfortunately, intuition is often denigrated as being inferior to logic, whereas strictly logical thinking can lock one into a rigid mold or system of beliefs.

People who choose to study and practice the mystical and magic arts often tread a scary path and choose to hide, as well as suppress, their visions and dreams. Both intuition and reason need to be recognized as viable methods of gaining knowledge. Hecate, who represents both learned wisdom and sudden, creative insight, can help us integrate these two sides of our nature so that neither one falls into the shadow and is denied.

Hecate also is useful in dealing with problems related to aging, death and the after life. In our society, the physical decay of the body and death are taboo subjects—so taboo that they break out in the constant barrage of gore in violent television and motion picture images. The modern insistence on looking young is one way of pushing the aging process into the shadow. To see violent death constantly in one's living room and on a small screen is one way to deny the reality of death. Hecate, as a goddess of death and regeneration, can help women and men realize that the death of the body is part of a natural process. As a crone figure, she emphasizes that as people age, they can retain their capabilities and good looks. Older persons, as well as younger ones, can turn to traditional natural healing methods such as using herbs to balance hormones and eating clean, organically-grown fruits and vegetables that provide minerals and vitamins. Ancient ways of massaging and working with the body help to keep it loose and flexible. Traditional Chinese Medicine and Ayurvedic Medicine from

India, both of which work with certain foods, herbs, and remedies, help us age easily and gracefully. The wisdom of the Crone means that one can return to earlier, more natural methods of healing, as well as using the methods of present-day medicine in a rational way.

We have been so bombarded by pictures of the withered old crone, toothless and bent over, that our inner vision of the aging woman is totally distorted. We are also bombarded by images of the very young as personifying the only desirable way to be and look. If we peruse some photographs of elder native women, as some of the Navajo and Hopi women in this country, the Huichol and Tarahumaras in Mexico, or photographs of older people by Imogen Cunningham and other photographers, we receive quite a different impression. In their faces we see beauty and wisdom, calm and balance. Needless to say, they are not worrying about osteoporosis or Estrogen Replacement Therapy; their aging is flowing in a way that is in harmony with nature and her cycles. More and more books today are written by and about older women. These women are not complaining, but instead talk about the benefits and changes that age brings. The beauty of the old is different from the beauty of the young; it does not lead to objectification of the body, but instead focuses on the spirit and personality of the subject.

Let us invoke Hecate, our Crone Mother, to dig out some of these fears from our unconscious, and transform them into new concepts that are in keeping with who we have become and how we are evolving. We know, even though the medical establishment doesn't seem to, that menopause is *not* a disease. And that hot flashes, although they can be balanced physiologically through herbs and supplements, are "power surges" reminding us of the red blood power that is within us. As the chant says, "We are the old women. We are the new women. We are the same women, wiser than before."

Hecate as an Archetype for Men as well as Women

All archetypes have two sides—spiritual and chthonic. Archetypes are never perceived in their actual form; they are seen through images that come from the unconscious and are essentially non-representational and can never be fully explained or disposed of. As a person grows older and becomes an individual, the shadow or dark side of any archetype must be consciously owned or honored.

For men, the wise old man has long been an honored archetype. Its

shadow is probably the silly, old fool or the old goat—but this is certainly not the way most men see themselves. The old witch, however, is a negative archetype within the collective unconscious. At one time women were honored as medicine women and looked up to by both sexes alike as carriers of the wisdom of the tribe. Today, the older woman is often dismissed or ignored. Getting in touch with Hecate will help men get in touch with their own mother, that is, their own roots. Men need to see that, insofar as the crone is part of the collective shadow, it needs to be recognized and dealt with. Neither the masculine nor feminine is complete without the other; and the feminine is the basis for the masculine as the mother is to the child. If a man can accept and understand the crone stage in women, he will better be able to come to terms with his own aging. As he recognizes his feminine, intuitive side, he will be more able to work and play creatively; he will be open to new experiences and systems.

Ritual for Invoking Hecate

Because we have discussed the multi-faceted Hecate mainly in two distinct ways, we will describe two possible rituals. These rituals should not be done on the same night. The first ritual relates to increasing and becoming comfortable with one's visionary powers.

Women should come to this ritual dressed in soft shades of dark purple, amethyst, or smoky blues. They can bring masks representing any of Hecate's many aspects and carrying her instruments—the key, the rope, or the dagger. Also, if possible, bring a crystal ball or glass bowl for scrying. Bring as many crystals as you wish to lay on the altar and use in the ritual.

The ritual should take place outdoors, if possible, with a cauldron in the middle set up so that the High Priestess or conductor of the ceremony can light a fire in it at the appropriate time.

After the area is smudged, an altar is set up in the middle of the circle, not far from the cauldron. On the altar may be placed owl wings, the crystals, branches from yew or poplar trees; an athame or sword, in the East; dark blue or purple candles in the south; owl wings or feathers in the West along with some water; and the crystal ball or glass bowl in the north.

To build up the energy, after the women are smudged, they may drum, rattle, and chant the following:

Hecate, Cerridwyn, Dark Mother, let me in.
Hecate, Cerridwyn, let me be re-born.[24]

The High Priestess invokes the four directions:

To the East we call in Artemis, virgin priestess, harbinger of a new dawn, a time when we can bring back the magic and be reborn.

To the South we call in Selene, bright Moon mother, bring us the passions and fruits, the sensuality of your luminous being.

To the West we call in all the priestesses of Hecate—Medea, Circe, and the others, take us into the dark underground and teach us the secrets of death and rebirth.

To the North we call in Hecate, Crone Goddess of the Dark Moon, to teach us your wisdom and your magic so that we might change and grow.

In the first part of the ritual, each woman shares how she has feared her visions and dreams, how she has either been afraid to follow them, or has, in fact, listened to them and what the results of doing so have been. She also shares how she has used any of the magical arts in her life—Tarot, astrology, numerology, crystal-gazing. Then take turns placing the crystals on different parts of each other's bodies or forehead and relate whatever visions or feelings come through. Every woman should experience having a crystal applied to some section of her body that she chooses, and be able to give herself up to the images brought by the crystal.

In the second part of the ritual, the crystal ball is brought forth and each woman takes a turn at scrying (looking into the ball and reading what she sees). All discuss the importance of their visions and their intention to follow them. The women then dance and drum, calling on the moon to inspire them with new ideas and visions.

The other ritual relates more to the shadow side of aging. Again the ritual should take place outdoors with a fire cauldron ready. This time the women dress primarily in black, bringing only a mask that represents Hecate in her Crone aspect and a staff or distaff. The altar should contain owl wings, branches from the black poplar or yew tree, and herbs such as mandragora and black poppy. Black candles in silver holders can be placed in the south, the athame in the East, owl wings or feathers in the West, and a picture of a wise, old woman in the north. The directions will be called in as in the first ritual.

If the women are all in the crone phase of life, they might discuss and celebrate what it means to be past the age of childbearing and menstruating. In particular, women can share how hormonal change has affected their sexual lives. Most women find at this period in life that sex becomes elective and less governed by the demands of their body. This freedom from the compulsiveness of the sexual urge is something the women can celebrate, along with the sensuality they still feel and enjoy. Since the crone stage is one where a woman can embark on quests that were formerly out of reach because of the usual female functions of childbearing, childrearing and housewifery, each woman can now turn her attention to inner questions and to ambitions that have not yet been realized. As wise women, each woman listens to the other with the "inner ear," that way of listening which tries to see beyond the false self to the core of the other person.

Next all the women spiral into the center, chanting Changing Woman. They each carry slips of paper on which they have written their fears relating to their own aging or death. One by one they burn the paper in the cauldron and shout out something as they do. The rest of the women answer "May it be so."

Chants and songs follow with feasting afterwards. The High Priestess asks everyone to eat seeds of the pomegranate if they are willing to return to the underworld with Hecate.

As usual, each ritual ends with the thanking of the four directions.

Changing Woman

There was a time before we were born
when we were the calm in the eye of the storm.
We had a memory, oh so deep, about the truth and the beauty so sweet
Man and a woman, passion run wild, they gave birth to a freedom child.
We are the children of love and light.
We will guide the planet through the perilous night.
There is a woman who weaves in the sky,
See how she spins, see her fingers fly.
She is the stardust from beginning to end.
She is our mother, our lover, our friend.
She is the weaver and we are the web,
She is the needle and we are the thread.
She changes everything she touches and everything she touches changes.
Changing woman, re-arranges. Changing woman, re-arranges.
Changes, touches, touches, changes.[25]

Personal Experiences with Hecate

Marcia:

I have been attuned to the presence of Hecate for many years, though I did not know her then as Hecate. When I was 29 years old, I discovered the profound and "mind-blowing" subject of astrology. Every question I had ever had about my life, what I was here for, why the last year had been such a nightmare (the Saturn return year), what my connections were with my parents, brother, ex-husband, soon fit into place. I never grappled with the "truth" of the information; it was all so apparent. When I started interpreting horoscopes, I used to look things up in books, the meaning of planets in certain houses, the aspects. This was still a safe way for me to work. Then a friend, who must have been Hecate's voice for me, said, "You're missing all the fun. Interpret it by yourself. Look at the books later." At first I was a bit afraid to do this—what did I know after only studying a couple of months?—but as I allowed myself to open this new door, I found that I knew a lot, so much that it was almost uncanny at times. That's when I felt the reality of reincarnation; I must have done this before or known these things.

The word "intuition" was just entering my vocabulary in a real way. I had never experienced what that meant, what it was like to have a flash of inspiration, or a flash that provided an idea that I knew I had never "learned." Later I realized that we all, women and men, have this gift of intuition, but that we have to use it to make it happen—like other talents it has to be trained. I had a very traditional college education, majoring in English Literature and writing hundreds of papers on literary criticism. I had never been taught to access my own intuition about what the poem or short story meant. It was always what this critic said or that critic.

Suddenly I was not only interpreting astrological horoscopes, but also beginning to read Tarot cards. This expanded and increased my intuitive faculties in an even stronger way, because there were no specifics in the cards the way there was in the horoscope. One had to go even deeper within oneself to ferret out their meanings.

Several years later a friend taught me how to use a pendulum. Though I fully believed in dowsing and the accuracy of the information, I didn't think I could do it. I took the pendulum home and felt I was getting all the wrong answers when I checked out my vitamin and mineral supplements to see if they were good for me. So I didn't use it for quite a while. Then a doctor friend, with whom I was working, demonstrated it to me again. This time I felt I could do it; something had changed within me and I was ready for this new tool. What resulted for me was a feeling of tremendous empowerment. I could access all the information that otherwise was not available to me. The pendulum enabled me to attune to many frequencies—foods to which people were allergic, supplements, herbs, homeopathic remedies, flower remedies, emotional complexes, past life work. As my practice with the pendulum increased, I was able to stop using the instrument itself, and begin dowsing in my mind. This was a farther step, again requiring some practice, and I didn't have to carry my pendulum with me!

In 1988 I conducted, along with several other women, the first Dark Goddess retreat at Isis Oasis in the heart of the wine country in Northern California. Although I was personally bringing through Pele at that retreat, one of my friends was doing Hecate. So through her, I began to have a feel for Hecate. After the retreat was over, I stayed an extra night. That night I had a most incredible dream. A wise, bearded old sage came to me and told me they had a house for me in Albany, CA, across the bay from where I was presently living in Marin County. He said it was so easy to find that I could even see it from my window. When I awoke, I was bewildered and somewhat amused by this dream. I had not been thinking of moving at all, at least consciously. In fact, I had not been thinking of making any changes in my life at that time (and yet our whole week-end was about the Dark Goddess and change). Something in my being said, "Follow this dream. It's something you've never done, had a visionary dream and followed it." Always I moved when I felt the change was necessary, or the stimulation to my own growth important. I had never acted on a dream before. And so I decided to look for the house and move. In fact, I did find the house very quickly; it was definitely the right house for me, only it was in El Cerrito (the town next to Albany). This experience gave me an even deeper trust in following dreams and visions. Years later, I realized that, in fact, Hecate (my friend who was bringing her through at the Retreat) was sleeping in the next room when I had the dream!

Gynne:

Although I have long been familiar with the concept of the unconscious, it has been very difficult for me to see how much I act out of my unconscious rather than my conscious self. In an earlier chapter I related the story of how I lost my car keys at the Dark Goddess retreat. Actually, whenever I am angry about going somewhere, I misplace my keys. Formerly, when I couldn't find my car keys, I would start searching frantically, throwing things around, dumping out my purse, taking cushions off the couch—in other words, making an angry mess without realizing I was angry. Now, when I misplace my keys, I stop, calm down, tell myself I am angry, and make a conscious decision either to go or stay home. Then, almost invariably, I immediately find my keys. I'm not quite sure what the keys symbolize—probably that I want to feel trapped into not having a choice. Certainly, the search is a way of diverting and dismissing my anger by focusing on the location of my keys. On another level, synchronicity played a large part in my key loss at the Dark Goddess workshop. I had known about the workshop from its inception and did all the advertising materials for the event. I thought I was looking forward to the ritual, and had thought a lot about my new crone name. One name I had come up with was Jeanie Giant Star because my birth name, Jean Riese Stern, means Jean Giant Star translated from German. The very fact that I had thought of such a jokey name for a ceremony I was looking forward to should have given me some clue about how ambiguous my feelings were.

When I arrived at the workshop all my critical, intellectual facilities were at work, while my psychic and heart chakras were closed to the size of a small slit. I felt like I was back at camp, which I hated as a child. While the idea of freely roaming wild animals was pleasant, I actively disliked their attendant flies.

I brought with me a red native dress I had bought in the *souk* at Jerusalem, so I could have impersonated Kali and Sekhmet had I known who either of these goddesses were. But, actually, since it was Halloween I was really in touch with Hecate, the crone.

A major part of being able to participate in a ritual is consent. And I didn't consent to the presence of the goddess. Despite the fact that my age made me more than eligible to be a crone, I wasn't ready to accept this stage of life—my rebellious and childish side came out. So I was rejected by Hecate, who was obviously the presiding deity at an All Hallows event. As a sign, I lost my key which is one of Hecate's three symbols—the key to the underworld and the knowledge of magic and the secrets of the afterlife. I wasn't ready to assume my place as a "wise woman" or to look at age and death with anything but aversion or scorn. It has taken me a long time to realize that I refused the gift of knowledge that was available at this workshop. I was fortunate enough to have been reminded by the goddess, but unable to see or understand what this reminder meant. I still haven't completely come to terms with the meaning of Hecate's key to the point where I can assume my cronehood with grace and wisdom; however, when one works with the goddess one realizes that although the message is given, first the message must be interpreted, and then its working out takes time and the willingness to change.

ENDNOTES

[1] Budge, E.W. in Walker, *Women's Encyclopedia of Myths and Secrets.* Page 378

[2] Larousse. *Encyclopedia of Mythlogy.* Page 38.

[3] Walker. Page 378.

[4] Mc Lean. Page 67.

[5] Larousse. Page 190.

[6] Graves, Robert. *The Greek Myths,* Vol I. Page 33.

[7] Larousse. See also Walker, page 379.

[8] Ibid.

[9] Walker. Page 379.

[10] Ibid.

[11] Mc Lean. Page 66.

[12] George, Demetra. *Mysteries of the Dark Moon.* Page 141.

[13] Graves, vol.1,31.7.

[14] George. Page 141.

[15] Graves. Page 124.

[16] Ibid.

[17] Mc Lean. Page 94.

[18] Graves, vol.1, 31.2

[19] George. Page 142.

[20] Graves. Page 125.

[21] Graves, vol.1, 31.5.

[22] Graves, vol. 1, 55 from Aristophanes' *Frogs, Parliament of Women;* Philostratus' *Life of Apollonius of Tyana* and others.

[23] Graves, vol.1, 55.1.

[24] from tape by Starhawk and the Reclaiming Collective

[25] from *The Goddess* tape, Sonoma Birth Collective

THE TRIPLE GODDESS:

Working With the Shadow

Invocation

Changeable
Challenging
Polarities disappear
In her three-faced presence

Decentered
Many dimensional
She confounds
    rigidity
     patriarchy
dissipating conflict

Three faces of the One
One face of the All
The Triple Goddess
Presides over
Life's eternal dance
Mixing shadow and light

I n the beginning was woman and she was three. She was the Moon Goddess who presided over the stages of life—generation, the spinner of the thread of life; growth, the measurer of the thread as it came off the spindle; and death, the cutting of the thread.

In the early Greek myths, we can easily understand the triple nature of the goddess. In the beginning there were three goddesses: Tethys who personified the sea, Nyx who was the sky or night, and Gaia, the earth. Gaia's children were the Olympian gods and goddesses including Zeus, Hera, and Demeter; they relate to the conscious mind. Tethys' children, arising from the sea, are different in character. They are at the interface of the conscious mind with the unconscious,[1] in other words, they are part of the subconscious. Tethys' children include Aphrodite, a Solar goddess, Metis (Medusa), and Europa (a Moon goddess identified with Hathor). Tethys is also the mother of the Gorgons, the Graeae, and the Sirens, all of whom stand at the threshold of the unknown. These three triplets are guardians beyond whom lie other, more fearsome, figures. They are either beautiful like the Sirens or once-beautiful like the Gorgons and the Graeae.

From Nyx come the darkest figures. Remember, Hecate is a daughter of Nyx. So are the three fates (Moirae), Nemesis ("due enactment" or the goddess who hates boastful words and brings destruction to the arrogant), the Erinyes (Furies), and the Hesperides. The daughters of Night lead us deep into our unconscious, but also stand as guardians to those of us who dare venture within. Hecate stands at the gateway to the underworld; the Erinyes protect the bloodlines of inheritance as passed on to future generations; and the Hesperides, standing at the Westernmost part of the world, guard our "inner need for immortality."[2]

In this book, we have talked exclusively of working with the dark goddesses, but only as a way of accessing that part of ourselves which is often buried. In order to achieve balance, it is also necessary to work with the Solar goddesses to fuse the Shadow with the Self.

The archetype of the triple goddess stands not only for phases in the life cycle of the person, but also of the planet. Some of the earliest interpretations of the triple goddess were that she stood for the three seasons of the year: planting, growing, harvesting. She also represents the three conditions of woman: maiden, mother, grandmother. The opera diva Frances Alda said in her biography, *Men, Women and Tenors* that women were either lovers, mothers or workers. In her trio, none of the archetypes is dark, although each have their dark aspect.

In Freudian terminology we can say the triple goddess stands for the id, the ego, and the superego. Here we have one conscious entity—the ego—and two unconscious or partly conscious (dark) entities. From the superego, insofar as it isn't acknowledged, comes repression. It is what women internalize as the "patriarchy"—that force which seems to come from without, but really comes from within the psyche, and oppresses. The superego can be more moral and better than the ego; it also can be "disembodied, airy, rigid, and anorectic."[3] From the unconscious id comes impulsive behavior, some of it harmful, some creative. It is the creative aspect of the id that caused Jung to say that the Shadow, although "closer to the animal and the instinctual… may be a superior part of the personality, a hidden talent."[4]

In the dark aspect of the triple goddess, we can discern the shadow side. "The shadow must threaten awareness… it comes in specific and unexpected moments."[5] When working with any of the dark goddesses in ritual, it is common for women to have sudden insights or bursts of suffering or feeling that are both painful and enjoyable. Although in ritual we work with the archetype (which represents a figure in the collective unconscious), for that archetype to be helpful, it must clue us into our own personal unconscious. The triple goddess is a Moon Goddess, lunar in nature. Working at night, under the light of the moon, allows women to confront their unconscious fears and desires in an indirect, sensitive and spiritual way, rather than in a harsh Solar glare which makes sharp distinctions between good and "evil."

The Christian god is exclusively masculine. Even the Assumption of Mary didn't change the masculine nature of the Christian trinity of God, the father; God, the son; and the Holy Spirit. In this theology, the Devil is perceived as having attributes considered feminine—he is serpentine, indirect, negative, and imperfect. Actually, the three aspects of God and the addition of the Devil make an interesting quaternity. The Devil combines the qualities considered by men to be feminine and "bad"; Christ has at least one quality considered feminine and "good"—the sacrificial nature of his being.

In the myths retold in this book, each dark goddess has her Solar counter part. But also, hidden behind both of these monumental figures, is a third woman—sometimes immortal, sometimes human—who encompassed what men would define as "good" female qualities. Lilith, the she devil, is opposed to the Shekina, the spiritual one. But then there is Eve. Poor Eve. She is human. She was perhaps not only the consort of Adam, but also a priestess of the great goddess because she was definitely connected with the serpent who knew what was forbidden to humans, the knowledge that should belong only to God(dess). When the serpent imparted this knowledge to Eve, she was expelled from Eden, became subject to death and given the pains of childbirth. And all this because she shared her knowledge with Adam, her spouse.

In the Inanna and Ereshkigal myth, Ghestianna, the sister of Dumuzi, displays love and compassion through sacrifice. Inanna condemned Dumuzi to life in the underworld without a pang, but Ghestianna gave up six months of her own life to take his place. Pele's sister, Hi'iaka, loyally undertook the dangerous and tedious journey to bring Pele's lover Lohiau to her, only to have Pele, out of distrust and jealousy, condemn both of them to be burned to death. Her immortality saved Hi'iaka from Lohiau's fate. In the Medusa story we are introduced to Andromeda, who is the embodiment of the hapless, but exquisite maiden, whose only function is to be rescued by the hero.

Kali, Sekhmet, and Hecate all come from older mythologies. All have their benevolent side, but at no point are they helpless or sacrificing. Sekhmet has a sister, Bast, who personifies Sekhmet in a lighter aspect—the cat as opposed to the lion; the goddess of love, joy and dancing as opposed to passion and lust. Kali can be the benevolent mother—Parvati is her virgin aspect so she can be innocent as well. Hecate was sometimes called the "lovely one" and part of her triple nature involved Artemis, the earthly virgin huntress; Selene, the Moon in Heaven; and Persephone, the goddess in the underworld. In her aspect as Persephone, Hecate can be considered the sacrificial rape victim. But Hecate is usually seen as a separate figure from Persephone—Persephone is Kore (the maiden) and Hecate the hag or crone.

The idea of the triple goddess leads to the hope that women can integrate their shadow with their conscious self so they can use the enormous power latent in both these sides. This integration should not be through becoming the martyr or the sacrificial victim. A long time ago, when Richard Nixon was president, a poll of women chose Pat Nixon and Jackie Kennedy as the most honored women in America because they "suffered." Suffering need no longer be a criteria on which women pride themselves. The repressed traits of the triple goddess—those traits personified in the dark goddesses—can show women how they can use their anger, sexuality, force of character and intellect. If women would marshall these qualities, there is no reason, as Dorothy Dinnerstein said in *The Minotaur and the Mermaid*, why women should not rule the world.

Gynne:

I don't know if I want to rule the world, but I do know that we need a more equal balance of power on the planet. The patriarchy has gotten out of hand and female energy is needed. The more I work personally with the Dark Goddesses, the more I tap into this energy for myself.

There are naturally negative sides to working with the dark goddesses. When Frances Alda divided women into mothers, lovers and workers I immediately categorized my mother as a "worker." I didn't want a mother who was a worker, I wanted a mother. But there is no reason why women cannot be all three without being either exhausted or frantic. Hecate gives us insight into our ability to work with the visionary, but to mistake illusion for reality is to leave oneself open to scorn and rejection by the practical world. Women, too, need to give men the right to enjoy some of those traits considered feminine. If we do not allow men to develop their spiritual and nurturing side, if we always expect them to be up and doing, how can we expect them not to be resistant to change in us?

Marcia:

When I first discovered the concept of the triple goddess it was very helpful and enlightening to me. It explained all the sides of my own nature that I experienced in childhood.

As a youngster, I spent much time alone; as a teenager, I shouldered a lot of responsibility in the years after my father died. People were always telling me I was an "old soul." In my twenties, in the theater, I was continually cast in the roles of older women. I had some gray hair even in my late twenties. I also played the mother part by cooking at home and taking care of my younger brother when my mother was forced to return to work.

It wasn't until my late twenties and early thirties, after my seven-year marriage ended, that I experienced my maiden part, which is light and airy, likes to dance, and is creative. The "hippie movement" of the 60s and living on Haight Street in San Francisco during 1967-68 were catalytic for me in uncovering my adolescence.

Now that I am a crone, past 50, I feel this maiden part is even stronger. I have more energy and creativity now than at any other time in my life.

Since I work as a healer and counselor, the mother part in me has always been strong, though I have learned to distance myself farther from that part and enjoy the creative wisdom of my crone years.

Maiden, mother, and crone—it is difficult to separate these three parts within myself—all are integral to my being.

ENDNOTES

[1] McLean, Adam. *The Triple Goddess*. Page 23.
[2] Ibid.
[3] Berry-Hillman, Patricia. "The Training of Shadow and the Shadow of Training." from the *Journal of Analytic Psychology*. Vol 26. Page 222.
[4] Ibid.
[5] Ibid. Page 223.

CONCLUSION

Marcia:

The Dark Goddess: Dancing with the Shadow has been a very special book for me to write. Though the book has reached its completion, my dance with the Dark Goddess and the Shadow is on-going. The research and reading I did in order to write this book have brought me into an even deeper relationship with each of the dark goddesses. As I focused on individual goddesses and invoked them to be with me while I wrote their story, many things happened in my own life. The people I saw in that time period, the places I went to, all were related to my work with that particular goddess. An example of this occurred the night before I started the Medusa chapter; I was taking a walk on some streets out in the country where I have been living, a walk I take almost every day. And there, right on the street was a beautiful snake skin. And so Medusa had entered my life at exactly the right time. The week I was the most thoroughly engrossed with Sekhmet I had several new clients call who had problems with addictive substances, as well as a visit from an old friend who also has had these problems. Each goddess brought me her magic and mystery and took me to a deeper level in my own psyche and my own unfolding spiritual path.

The most exciting part, however, has been to conduct rituals for each of the goddesses with women who are sincerely working on their own transformation. For these women and the way the goddesses manifested through them, I am extremely grateful. In doing a ritual for Lilith, and in speaking of her myth as a child killer, one woman was taken back to the time when her own child died and was able to release a tremendous amount of grief that she still carried. After a Kali ritual there was much discussion of mother/daughter relationships, how to handle being a "terrible mothers" and the rage women tell towards their own children. During a ritual invocation of Hecate, two women broke down in tears remembering a time in their childhood when they were forced to have some birthmarks removed from their bodies. Different energies evoke different memories and one never knows what a particular goddess will elicit.

To work with these dark goddesses in ritual in whatever way speaks to you as a reader of this book will provide a challenge and will no doubt add much depth and richness to your life. If we have stimulated you sufficiently to do this work, then our goal in writing this book has been accomplished. As authors and as ritualists working with the Dark Goddess, we send you our special blessings. May the Dark Goddess fill you with her awe and mystery!

Gynne:

Writing a book is always a learning experience. *The Dark Goddess: Dancing With the Shadow* I discovered through research the interrelation of world cultures. I was brought up in a Jewish family and attended Sunday School when I was a child. I saw the Jewish religion as something apart from all other systems of belief. I think I was taught to look at Judaism that way — that the Hebrews were the first, and the only true, monotheists. Of course, I knew that Christ was Jewish and that Christianity sprung from Judaism, but the history or mythology we learned in Sunday School ended long before the coming of Christianity.

Recently, as a much older person, I have been working with the goddesses in ritual. But it was only when I began researching Lilith in Raphael Patai's *The Hebrew Goddess* that I began to understand that Jews worshipped goddesses and other gods as well as El or Yahweh. I remembered that I never understood why those ancient Hebrews seemed so concerned over worshipping a golden calf. I had no idea of the significance of the golden calf or its relation to the goddess-based religions of the Near East. Nor did I understand the history of the serpent in the story of Adam and Eve. Most important, however, I had no idea that Jews, right up until the historic period and beyond, worshipped a goddess similar to Astarte and had figures of her in their temples; nor had I heard of the female spiritual principle, the Shekina. I began to discover that not only had most early peoples worshipped a female deity before a male one became supreme, but that goddess worship has never really died out. All over the world, the female was seen and still is seen as the fundamental spiritual originator of all life just, as woman is known as the biological originator of the human baby.

I began to find working in ritual with the goddesses more meaningful than before. Using the dark goddesses to help women get in touch with less accessible parts of their personalities was a very fruitful way to allow expression of feelings not usually acknowledged. I felt a great kinship with Ereshkigal, in particular. And I saw how I had buried the Inanna part of myself. In some way, Ereshkigal is the quintessential martyr, always moaning and groaning about her "inside" and her "outside." I decided to work personally with Inanna both in ritual and through study and meditation. As a result I have become more active in my life and less of a complainer.

I hope this book encourages many women to work with the dark goddesses (and certainly also the solar ones). The power of ritual has brought magic and richness into my life and I hope it will into yours as well. May the Goddess be with you as you walk the path of life.

BIBLIOGRAPHY

Beckwith, Martha *Hawaiian Mythology*. Honolulu, HI: University of Hawaii Press, 1987.

Berry-Hillman, Patricia. "The Training of the Shadow and the Shadow of Training." From *The Journal of Analytic Psychology*, Vol. 26.

Boswell, John. *Christianity, Social Tolerance & Homosexuality*. University of Chicago Press, 1981.

Budge, E. A. Wallis. *The Egyptian Religion*. New York, NY: Bell Publishing Co., 1959.

Budge, E. A. Wallis. *The Gods of the Egyptians*. Vol I. New York, NY: Dover, Inc., 1969.

Bulfinch, Thomas. *The Age of Fable*. New York, NY: New American Library, 1962.

Downing, Christine. *Goddesses: Mythological Images of the Feminine*. New York, NY: Crossroad Press, 1981.

Estes, Clarissa Pinkola, Ph.D. *Women who Run with the Wolves*. New York, NY: Ballatine Books, 1992.

Freud, Sigmund. *Collected Papers*. Vol. 5. New York, NY: Basic Books, 1959.

Garrison, Omar. *Tantra: The Yoga of Sex*. New York, NY: Harmony Books, 1983.

Gadon, Elinor W. *The Once and Future Goddess*. San Francisco, CA: HarperCollins, 1990.

George, Demetra. *Mysteries of the Dark Moon*. San Francisco, CA: HarperCollins, 1992.

Gimbutas, Marija. *The Language of the Goddess*. San Francisco, CA: HarperCollins, 1989.

Gimbutas, Marija. *The Civilization of the Goddess*. San Francisco, CA: HarperCollins, 1991.

Goodrich, Norma Lorre. *Priestesses*. New York, NY: HarperCollins, 1989.

Graves, Robert. *The Greek Myths*. Vol.1 & 2. Baltimore, MD. Penguin Books, 1955.

Griffin, Susan. *Pornography and Silence*. San Francisco, CA: HarperCollins, 1981.

Hamilton, Edith. *Mythology*. New York, NY: New American Library, 1940.

Harrison, Jane Ellen. *Prolegomena to the Greek Religion*. New York, NY: Meridian Books, 1955.

Ions, Veronica. *Egyptian Mythology*. London: Hamlyn House, 1965.

Jacobsen, Thorkild. *The Sumerian King List*. Chicago, IL. 1939.

Jung, C.G. "Four Archetypes" translated by R.F.C Hull, from *The Collected works of C.G. Jung*, Vol. 9, part 1, Bollingen Series, XX.

Jung, C. G. *Symbols of Transformation*. from The Collected Works of C. G. Jung, Vol V. Bollingen Series.

Jung, Emma. *Animus and Anima*. Dallas, TX: Spring Publications, 1957.

Junker, Howard (Ed). *Roots & Branches: Contemporary Essays by West Coast Writers*. San Francisco, CA: Mercury House, 1991.

Kane, Herb Kawainui. *Pele—Goddess of Hawaii's Volcanoes*. Captain Cook, HI: Kawainui Press, 1987.

Kasl, Charlotte Davis, Ph.D. *Women, Sex and Addiction*. New York, NY: Tichnor & Fields, 1989.

Kelly, Marion. *Pele and Hi'iaka.* Bishop Museum Publications. Honolulu, HI: Bishop Museum Press, 1984.

Koltuv,Barbara Black. *The Book of Lilith.* York Beach, ME: Nicholas Hays, Inc., 1987.

Larousse Encyclopedia of Mythology. New York, NY: Prometheus Press, 1960.

Masters, Robert. *The Goddess Sekhmet.* Amity, NY: Amity House, 1988.

Mc Lean, Adam. *The Triple Goddess.* Grand Rapids, MI: Phanes Press, 1989.

Miller, Milton, M.D. *Nostalgia: A Psychoanalytic Study of Marcel Proust.* Boston, MA: Houghton Mifflin, 1956.

Mookerjee, Ajit. *Kali The Feminine Force.* New York, NY: Destiny Books, 1988.

Neumann, Erich. *The Great Mother.* Trans. by Ralph Manheim, Bollingen Series XLVII. Planckton, NJ: Princeton University Press, 1974.

Newman, Ernest. *Wagnerian Nights.* London: Pan Books, 1949.

Niethammer, Carolyn. *Daughters of the Earth.* New York, NY: Macmillan, 1977.

Patai, Raphael. *The Hebrew Goddess.* Detroit, MI: Wayne State University Press, 1978.

Patrick, Richard. *The All Color Book of Egyptian Mythology.* Hong Kong: Octopus Books, 1972.

Perera, Sylvia Brinton. *Descent to the Goddess.* Toronto, Canada: Inner City Books, 1981.

Scholem, Gershom. *Origins of the Kabbalah.* Trans. by Allan Arkush. Planckton, NJ: Princeton University Press, Jewish Publication Society, 1990 (1st printed 1962).

Stein, Diane. *Casting the Circle—A Women's Book of Ritual.* Freedom, CA: Crossing Press, 1990.

Stone, Merlin. *Ancient Mirrors of Womanhood.* Boston, MA: Beacon Press, 1979.

Walker, Barbara. *The Crone.* San Francisco, CA: HarperCollins, 1985.

Walker, Barbara. *The Woman's Encyclopedia of Myths and Secrets.* San Francisco, CA: HarperCollins, 1983.

Wolkstein, Diane and Kramer, Samuel. *Inanna, Queen of Heaven and Earth.* San Francisco, CA: HarperCollins, 1983.

Woodman, Marion. *Addiction to Perfection.* Toronto, Canada: Inner City Books, 1982.

Yalom, Irvin D., M.D. *Love's Executioner.* New York, NY: Basic Books, 1989.

INDEX